Praise for No B

"How surprised would you be to find out one of the giants of advertising has penned a memoir of true stories about his personal Don Quixote jousts? All I can say is you shouldn't be. With such an illustrious career you can imagine that David Altschiller must have more than his share of them. He does and like the man himself, David Altschiller's *No Business for Adults* is a charming, intelligent and yes, funny recollection of years of dealing with idiocy, both expected and unexpected. In the case of the latter, you'll want to read the chapter on Mae West. Brilliant!"

— Jeff Gorman, Retired Copywriter, Retired TV Commercial Director and Active Un-Paid Uber Driver to two adult non-driving kids

"David Altschiller, unlike many of advertising's self-congratulatory icons, is a practitioner whose work made the brands he partnered with more famous than he made himself.

David has always been effortlessly charming, piercingly insightful and great fun as you'll discover in this chronicle of advertising's light (and often ironic) side. But don't let David's comic timing fool you. His point of view is from a mountain of accomplishments."

— Andy Berlin, illustrious advertising refugee

"If you wanna read how the great ads of the 1960s and '70s, the golden age of advertising, came about; how the infighting, cutthroat competitiveness and sheer creative brilliance of the young Italian and Jewish artists and writers off the streets of Brooklyn and the Bronx grabbed the business away from the cautious, ivy league, buttoned up suits; how these creatives used chutzpah and gamblers' instincts to convince clients that irony, gallows humor, reverse psychology, and deep human insights and heart would sell their product, then get David Altschiller's memoir."

— Stan Mack, creator of "Real Life Funnies" in *The Village Voice*, "Out-takes" in *Adweek* magazine, and "Real Mad" in *Mediapost*.

"Don Draper, move over. For the skinny on advertising's 'Golden Age,' I'll take David Altschiller any day. With stories ranging from hilarious to horrifying, his memoir is a witty, revealing chronicle of 'Mad Ave.' and its counterparts from the '60s through 2000s. We get behind-the-scenes peeks at the celebrity pitchmen and pitchwomen Altschiller worked with and a glimpse of Altschiller explaining a risqué radio script to queen-of-the-risqué Mae West. But this book is much more than a series of vivid moments. It's a reminder of why we need to support true creativity wherever it's found — including in this indelible memoir."

—Melissa Balmain, author of *The Witch Demands a Retraction*

No Business for Adults

No Business for Adults

Adults

My Life in Advertising

David Altschiller

ISBN: 978-1-947635-43-2 (Hardcover Edition)
ISBN: 978-1-947635-42-5 (Paperback Edition)
ISBN: 978-1-947635-44-9 (Ebook Edition)

First Printing October 2021

Published by Barnard Bookworks
For more information, visit www.davidaltschiller.com

Contents

Introduction

I was a Mad Man—for real.

I lived through the transitions from early television advertising to the unimagined power of the internet. I experienced, first-hand, wonderful, and terrible days at the very best and the very worst agencies. I worked for notorious monsters. I also worked with some of the most creative people in the history of the business. I wrote commercials for celebrities who were impossibly difficult and some who were charming beyond knowing.

I was fortunate enough to work in what they call the "Golden Age" of advertising. And even more fortunately, I was able to work at one of the agencies that made the age golden. I was able to parlay this experience into an agency of my own that I led for 25 years. I'll take you back to all those places with me.

This book is written, hopefully, more about the business than about me. My attempt here is to give you a sense of what the advertising business was and is—really is.

From *The Hucksters* in 1947 to *The Man in the Grey Flannel Suit* in 1956 to *Mad Men* in 2007, television and movies have always painted a distorted picture of the advertising business—both positively and negatively. My hope is to un-glamorize the ugly and foolish, to laud the laudable, and bring some of sense reality to it all. The business is both better and worse than you've been led to believe.

For those wanting an honest portrayal of the business over the last 50 years, it is a glimpse at the unvarnished truth—at least from my point of view. In short, my goal for this book is to provide the reader a rare look behind the gilded curtains.

My Life Before Advertising

SINCE this not an autobiography, I will race through my early life and quickly get to the subject of advertising. Which, I imagine, is why you bought the book.

From the time I was 4 or 5 years old, it was clear what I was going to be when I grew up. I was going to be a doctor. The idea garnered great support from my family. You see, I am Jewish. When you're Jewish, "my son, the doctor," is not a Henny Youngman joke. It is the consummate career, the ultimate source of pride. Remember, growing up in America in the mid-20th century, Jewish parents never dreamed their son could be President. They still don't.

Like other children, as far back as I can remember, my goal was making my parents proud. Unlike many other parents, mine were easily satisfied. I've spoken to friends who'd tell me that they never were good enough in their parents' eyes, no matter how well they performed. Not so with my folks. They told me I was the best and smartest as early as I could walk. And I believed them. They thought so much of me, I came to think I could accomplish almost anything.

I did my best not to disappoint them. I did so well in primary and middle school that I skipped several grades. At age 13, I took an exam for a specialized science high school in New York. It was an all-boys school, so being so much younger than my schoolmates was not as problematic as it might have been had there been girls around. After science high school, I went through four years of pre-med majoring in biology, minoring in English. I loved literature. I hated chemistry and physics. Despite this, I persevered and got into medical school and pretty quickly came to realize that being a doctor was, from the beginning, my parent's career choice, not mine. I was convinced that my confessing this to them would be the darkest day of their lives. They responded, "So what else do you want to do?" Huh? I had thoroughly misunderstood, over all those years, that their love was for me, not medicine. I thought I was giving them what they wanted. They thought they were giving me what I wanted. What a waste of biology books. As it turns out, I was born to write ads, not prescriptions. If only I'd dealt with the issue more honestly.

After giving up what I thought was my lifetime ambition, I could have chosen between the sciences (other than medicine) or things related to English. But what?

At this point, I was very tired of biology and chemistry. I had always hated physics. So, I went on to graduate school in English. Along the way, it became apparent to me that teaching English was not the right path, either. The limited experience I had in teaching made it clear. It deeply insulted me that that I cared much more about literature than my students did. They were busy sleeping off the previous night.

(Later in life, I spent part of every summer for 25 years teaching advertising to working creative people in the master's program at Syracuse University. Unlike my first experience with disinterested and unfocussed young people, this experience with fully engaged adults who were eager to learn was one of the most rewarding of my life.)

But what could I do at this point with my English background besides teaching? Publishing? Public relations? Personnel? Advertising? As a child, I loved jingles and could sing all of them, but I truly knew nothing about advertising. Honestly, I had no clue about anything.

In a conversation with a friend, he suggested I become a copywriter. What caused him to come to this conclusion, I never asked. Since he probably had no good reason, it's a good thing I didn't inquire.

What did a copywriter do? I really had little idea. But it sounded creative, and at least as good as my other not-thought-out career choices, so why not?

Thus, after a lifetime of preparing for a career in medicine, I chose a life path blindly. How does one make a career decision on a whim? Simple: I didn't think it was a career decision. I thought it was a job. I had an even better excuse: I was very young. I had a lifetime of mistakes in front of me.

(I always thought a great addition to a middle school/high school curriculum would be a course called "What Do People *Really* Do For a Living?" This would be a video series based on the daily lives of doctors, accountants, plumbers, auto mechanics, truck drivers, computer programmers, chefs, lawyers, architects, etc. How do they prepare for their jobs? What do they really do for 8 hours a day? What sense of accomplishment they feel? If only young people could base their life choices on something more than whimsy or misinformation.)

But let us get back to me. Utterly fearless, directionless, and armed only with my ignorance, I set out to find a copy trainee position. Somehow, I got one and put one foot in front of the other for the next 40 years. I was lucky. I made a grossly uninformed choice and it turned out to be one that gave me a life better than I could have ever planned.

You should note that the first 3 agency jobs I had were: terrible, even worse, and vaguely decent. But hang on — things get better.

The Terrible Early
Ad Years

Benton and Bowles

PURSUING my new direction in life, I answered an ad in the New York Times for an opening in the creative training program at Benton and Bowles (B&B), one of the larger and more prestigious ad agencies in New York City. At that time, New York was the center of the advertising universe. Miraculously, I got the job. After a short while, I came to understand why I got the job so easily. It was the first advertising misrepresentation I encountered.

My place in the B&B creative training program was housed in the accounting department. Accounting? You read that right. Rather than learning how to write a headline or a script for a TV spot, I spent my days adding up endless columns of numbers as a media estimator. This, they suggested, was preparing me to be a copywriter. Had they advertised a job as "media estimator," I might be a dentist today.

About a month after I arrived in numeric hell, a monumental event happened at the agency. Crest Toothpaste, one of Proctor and Gamble's major brands at B&B, received the American Dental Association (ADA) Seal of Approval. Holy cavity, this was big news!

The media department at B&B — the department that decides where and when advertising runs — decided that Crest should run a full-page ad announcing the ADA's landmark endorsement in each and every newspaper in the entire U.S. This may have been the largest single one-day print campaign in ad history, to date. It was my pleasant job to figure out the cost of each of those ads. Do you know The Pasco, Tri-City Herald? The Pocatello Gazette? The Portsmouth Herald? I didn't, but I was suddenly on speaking terms with all of them.

There were no computers to accomplish this bookkeeping nightmare back then; there was me and my adding machine. I had to look up each paper's per-line advertising rate in a massive book called *Standard Rate and Data*, determine whether Crest had earned any discounts for running all its advertising to date, and add the new full-page line totals to establish the new discounted costs.

When I was done with weeks of this tedium, I sent the totals to the media department who, in turn, sent them to the Crest people who, in turn, decided that the total cost was far too expensive.

"Jeez, it costs *that* much?"

When they set out to buy a full-page ad in every newspaper in the country, you'd think that they'd have some idea of the expense. In the end, one look at the bottom line made it clear they'd have to cut some papers from the list. This meant that they'd lose their newly earned discounts and I was forced to recalculate the whole thing from scratch. This was definitely not a creative endeavor.

However, there was one very creative person in the department — my boss, Al Ferrarese. Mr. Ferrarese masterminded the largest embezzlement in the history of the advertising industry to date.

Listen to this creative brilliance: He opened a bank account in the name of William Morris (Isn't that the same as that of the giant talent agency? You bet it is.). He then deposited various client checks that came to the agency directed to the William Morris agency into his own "William Morris" account to the tune of $2 million. Is this brilliant or what? He then spent it in creative ways: Broadway show tickets, box seats at Yankees games, and lavish lunches for everyone he ever knew. He was brilliant at thinking up ways to be a big spender. This was the most generous guy you'd ever meet, but he was spending someone else's money. It took some time for the agency to uncover his magnanimity, and a lot of effort to minimize the negative press that would expose the agency's lack of oversight. I understand that the number of fraudulent activities that are swept under the rug to avoid corporate humiliation are quite numerous

Alas, I was not inclined to be brilliant in embezzlement. Instead, once every 2 months, I'd march — actually crawl — into the

Personnel Department and beg to know when I might be transferred to the Creative Department.

"As soon as there's an opening," they'd say. There never was one. I was so good at media estimating, why change things?

Just about a year into this bad dream, I was playing softball for the B&B team and one of our players tripped over first base and broke his leg. I helped the fellow, Dick Lord, from Central Park to Lenox Hill Hospital. Had he not been such a klutz, I never would have met him, and my real creative career might never have begun.

"So what do you do at the agency, David?" Dick asked me, between moans, while in the cab on the way to the hospital.

"Well, I'm in the creative training program."

"That's odd, I'm Creative Director and I have no idea who you are or what that is."

So much for the creative training program.

"Come down to my office tomorrow, and maybe we can make something happen," Dick said.

And it did.

Dick gave me my start. He showed me what an ad was and what it wasn't. Over the months, he encouraged me at my feeble attempts and was genuinely supportive and helpful. I am forever grateful.

One thing I've learned is that most people who have gotten anywhere had a mentor. Dick was my first. I've had several since and I've never forgotten them.

I've mentored many others over the years. It's not simply about paying my mentors back. I recognize that it doesn't take much to change someone's life. When you're Jewish, you're told there are no pearly gates. Your immortality is the effect you have on others during your time on Earth. There were so many good people who have helped me get to where I am; mentoring others is the least I can do.

I stayed at B&B for six more months working with Dick and putting a portfolio together. Once it was finished, I knew it was time to leave. Had I stayed there, I would have been known as "the guy from the accounting department pretending to be a writer," which would be worse than starting at the bottom. Armed with a portfolio filled with speculative ads for Parliament Cigarettes, Pampers, Crest, and Mutual of New York, I set out for the new world.

Norman, Craig, and Kummel

I took my portfolio to one of the multitudes of employment agents that specialized in advertising. Amazingly, with my meager array of speculative ads, I landed a job as a junior copywriter. Wow! I was not a trainee but an actual junior copywriter. I should have understood with my sketchy portfolio of speculative ads that the agency that hired me would be sketchy, too. In fact, I came to learn that it was, without question, one of the most notorious agencies of its time—Norman, Craig, and Kummel (NCK). Notorious? Really? Yes, and you'll soon understand why.

NCK was dominated by a larger-than-life personality by the name of Norman B. Norman. Norman Norman? Really? Of course not. That wasn't his real name. His birth name was Norman Weinstein. Norman, the person, was as manufactured as his moniker.

In advertising, like so many other fields, Jews had been long excluded from entry. As a result, there was only one way to break into fields like law, banking, and public relations—start your own firm. And that's what dozens of enterprising Jews did. Norman's career began at an agency started by one such entrepreneur, Milton Biow.

These agencies functioned in an alternative universe to the mainstream Protestant agencies that boasted large automotive or industrial business clients. Often these "Jewish agencies" had fashion and retail clients in abundance. No surprise. These were fields that Jews dominated, so why not take your business to a Jewish run agency?

Norman rose quickly at Biow and then opened his own agency. Over time, he fashioned himself after one of his more infamous clients, Charles Revson, the head of Revlon. There are books written on Revson (*Fire and Ice*) and there should be books written about Norman. Revson was tall and thin, wore blue pin-striped suits, and was famously abusive to his employees. Norman was tall and thin, wore blue pin-striped suits, and was a wannabe monster.

This was 1963. Truly the age of Mad Men, and these guys weren't just mad, they were often obscenely cruel. The TV show *Mad Men* had some difficult characters, but few could rival the nastiness and bullying of Revson and Norman.

At NCK, in every office and cubicle there was a little woodblock sign with the agency slogan "EMPATHY" emblazoned on it. It glared at you every time you sat down. Early in Norman's advertising career, he was involved in research and believed that the commercials his agency created were the result of a deep, emotional understanding of the human condition. If you saw the commercials, you'd be hard pressed to make the connection. The ads were more claptrap than representative of real, human emotion. To me, the word "obnoxious" or perhaps "offensive" would have been more appropriate on the woodblock sign.

To prove just how empathic the agency was, in every office there was also a speaker phone that had a direct line to Norman's office. A direct line? Really! Imagine how special you would feel with access to the boss! Except it was a one-way speaker phone from the boss to you. Should that phone blink on with an incoming call, you'd run out of your office as fast as your legs could carry you. Because when that voice was heard, you knew you were in big trouble. (Mercifully, I was too far down the totem pole to ever receive such a call.)

Empathy was antithetical to the way the agency functioned. People were fired almost every Friday. Those of us who were lucky enough to remain employed were asked to work the weekend.

Peter Gross somehow learned that he was going to be fired one Friday. Brilliant guy that he was, he simply didn't show up that day. He figured, "If I'm not here, you can't fire me." Wrong. Undaunted in their unholy task, folks from the personnel department loaded a van with the contents of his office and deposited it all on his lawn in Larchmont over the weekend. Included, was a note outlining the terms of his dismissal and two weeks' pay. The grim reaper didn't have a more efficient system. You couldn't hide from them, just like "Dirt can't hide from intensified Tide." (Another deathless slogan from P&G at the time.)

At places like NCK, life was far uglier than anyone could invent on *Mad Men*. Viewers and critics would reject this excessive ugliness as not credible. But if you were living in the middle of it, you wouldn't classify it as cruel or ruthless, you'd simply call it the business of advertising.

This brings to mind a more despicable tale. Jack Goldstein was a sweet guy working as an art director at a small fashion agency. The owner of the agency was, like Norman, not exactly Mr. Nice Guy. He was planning to fire Jack on Friday, but Jack was taken to the hospital on Thursday for an emergency appendectomy. This disrupted the owner's plans. Jack would be in the hospital for at least a week, collecting pay, and using medical benefits. The owner saw this as a waste of salary and benefits on someone who was going to be fired the instant he got back. Somehow, he tracked Jack down as he lay on a gurney bound for surgery.

"Hello, Jack?"

"Huh," Jack answers; already half under anesthesia.

"Jack, this'll just take a minute... Jack?"

"Huh?" says Jack. "Can you call me back? They're wheeling me into surgery.

"Jack, this'll just take a sec, Jack. We have to let you go. You know how these things are. It's not you. You're a great guy. It's just that... well, things are a little tight. But don't worry, you'll have your two weeks' pay waiting for you when you get home from the hospital. Good luck on the table."

That's the way things were. NCK was not unique in its brutality.

Joe Marco was the copy chief at NCK. This made him second only to the Creative Director. One very odd thing about Joe Marco — the copy chief of the entire agency — was that he worked on a freelance basis. How is it that the second most senior creative officer in the company, the man in charge of running the entire staff of the creative department, was not on staff himself? It baffles me to this day. (This was before agencies cheated creative staffs out of health benefits by making them work freelance. Agencies were at the vanguard of this movement.) So, what was the reason behind keeping Joe off staff? Perhaps to keep him on his toes?

Although, I imagine it's hard to come off your toes at an agency where they fire people every Friday.

Joe was an amazing combination of New York City street-smart Italian and brilliant academic. Reciting Chaucer in Middle English flawlessly, Joe was the essence of the ethnic underclass that was entering the ad business for the first time. He was educated but unpolished, remarkably smart, and shrewd.

Up to this point, the creative department, like the rest of the business, was populated by Ivy League Protestants. Their most important attribute was that they had grown up with other Protestants who were now their clients.

But the world was changing, and a generation of Joe Marcos were entering the industry. With the birth of a handful of enlightened creative agencies, Jewish copywriters and Italian art directors were displacing the "creative suits." The account management staff was still solidly Protestant, but now, to the eternal benefit of the industry, the "suits" were expected to sell, not create. Creative advertising was being handed over to people who were actually creative.

A sad and interesting sidebar: When Joe Marco died, in his obituary there was a glowing discussion of his most famous creative achievement. The "White Knight" was a hero in full armor galloping down the street on his noble white steed. His lance had the power of Ajax laundry detergent to turn clothes sparkling white with a zap. (This was supposed to be empathy, I guess. Our hero must have starred in millions of housewives' dreams.)

The fact is, Joe didn't create the "White Knight." Oh, he approved it and sold it to the client, but a cub writer like me wrote it. I guess because Joe presented it, he felt he had the right to take credit for creating it. At NCK, even the origin of your crowning achievement was questionable. It was indicative of the agency — everybody stole from everybody, and nobody was allowed creative ownership over anything.

These were the days when young creative people like me were expendable. Every day, we filled reams of cheap, yellow paper with hundreds of headlines for our creative supervisors to pick through and choose from. The supervisors created little. They weren't nearly as creative as their bevy of underpaid underlings. They wouldn't deign to waste their time fighting for the work. We gave them the raw material from which they could impress the client without threatening the client. They went to the meetings, were articulate and presentable, and we were invisible.

I was permitted to attend one client meeting while at NCK and I remember it quite vividly. You would, too.

I was expected to have no speaking part in the meeting but was simply there to observe and learn on the off chance I actually might be allowed to speak one day. The meeting was with Charles Revson. Why they chose to put a novice in a meeting with Mr. Revson still puzzles me. Revson was known for his strong opinions and uncharitable behavior. At this meeting, I saw evidence of this first-hand.

About 20 minutes into the meeting, Revson stopped the discussion abruptly.

"I've noticed," he said as he turned to a group of us, "that there are one, two, three, four, five people in the room who've made no contribution to this meeting whatsoever. You, you, you, you, and you... I'd like you to leave... Now!" And with that, I rose along with my four silent compatriots in utter humiliation and left. No one else from the agency seemed appalled or even fazed. I guess this was part of the standard operating procedures. In my remaining time at NCK, I was never in a room with Revson again. I felt no sense of loss.

At NCK, writers and art directors did not work together in teams. It took the upstart creative agencies like Doyle Dane Bernbach (DDB) to recognize that people with a visual sense and people with a verbal sense might actually complement each other. Together, they might reach places they couldn't get to on their own. I had to go to another agency to experience this enlightened place.

At traditional agencies like NCK, art directors were often farther down the creative food chain than copywriting juniors. They were simply "hands" — folks who would draw visual ideas that would accompany the headline they were given. If we were creating a print ad, copywriters would slip our supervisor-approved headlines under the door, and art directors would supply the visual sketches to go with them. This is an important distinction. It meant that ads were copy-driven, but rarely visually-driven.

In television, the art director's role was even more diminished. Copywriters created the audio scripts and the visual directions and the art directors would draw cartoon storyboards of the visual cues they had been given. Eventually, they were permitted to contribute creatively. Still, at most mainstream agencies, it was several more years before they were seen as valuable creative contributors.

Even more soul-crushing than the art director/copywriter relationship, NCK had devised a formula for creating commercials that was creatively numbing. The agency was the industry's originator of the visual pun.

A writer created a slogan and then the slogan was literally visualized. And I do mean literally.

Consider, "Let Hertz put you in the driver's seat." A man flies through the sky and lands in the seat of convertible without impaling his gonads on the steering column. Get it? The man is literally *put* in the driver's seat.

For Ajax All-Purpose Cleaner, an announcer intones, "Ajax cleans like a white tornado." Guess what happens next? A white tornado suddenly emerges from the box, whirls around, and makes your house sparking clean. Brilliant, huh? This bit of advertising magic was called a mnemonic device — a visual key to remembering the slogan forever.

Consider this NCK classic: "I dreamed I went to blazes in my Maidenform bra." This was a real ad complete with a busty model in a bra, oh, and a fire hat. Suggestive? Stupid? This was not just one ad, but part of a campaign that ran for years. "I dreamed I flew a kite," "I dreamed I swayed the jury," "I dreamed I barged down the Nile." This may seem like the advertising dark ages today, but NCK took this stuff to the bank. The formula was dazzlingly successful. Even ladies' underwear was not safe.

This drivel was making gobs of money for the agency and garnering all sorts of publicity. For me, it was making me suicidal.

I would lie awake at night, angrily inventing slogans using the formula.

For Maidenform — "I dreamed I was the Statue of Liberty..."

For Ex-lax — "Take a flying shit." Good visual, huh?

For Trojans — "Oh, come now!"

Anyone can do it.

My imagined off-color slogans kept me sane, and I knew I had to stay sane long enough to get bona fide packaged goods credentials — albeit via utterly dreadful commercials.

There were a host of very bright creative people slogging along with me at NCK. Many became brainwashed and spent their entire careers at the packaged goods agencies; their work doomed to live in the morass of mediocrity. They were paid big bucks for the awfulness they created. These were otherwise exceptionally intelligent people who "drank the Kool-Aid." (Note that this was before Jim Jones' mass suicide popularized the phrase.)

For creatives at NCK, work was an exercise in self-deception. If you acknowledged how terrible the work was, you couldn't look yourself in the eye. Instead, you focused on how successful the commercial was, or how much money you were making, or how wonderful it was to live in Darien. And then, as if you had swallowed two Anacin, the pain went away. I was never as proficient at this type of self-deception. I knew the work was crap. It ate at me and I dreamed of getting out.

A year into the NCK gig, a light bulb went on that I couldn't ignore. One of my co-workers jogged up to me on the street outside the office at lunchtime and excitedly announced, "David, I just heard two sentences of the Ajax script that you wrote about six months ago. They're in the latest spot that's on the air right now! Both sentences!" He slapped me on the back. "Congratulations!" This was the product of my year's work. Two sentences.

I suddenly came face to face with reality. The only work that I had written in my time at the agency that had appeared on television was a couple of inane lines buried in a mediocre commercial. At that moment, I had a long-delayed revelation: I could not stay another day at NCK.

I knew that my decision to join this dreadful agency in the first place had been a necessary one. I recognized that the big, awful, packaged goods experience would open doors. At some agencies, packaged goods know-how was a magical credential. But I knew that I couldn't work at another big, packaged goods agency ever again. It is hard to be embarrassed by what you do every day, especially if everyone around you isn't embarrassed. You are forced to live the awful truth alone.

I left NCK with almost nothing I was proud of to add to my port-folio, but I had an important credential — I had actually worked as a real copywriter at a major agency. What's more, I also worked on prestigious, packaged goods TV commercials. Most importantly, I learned some valuable lessons about all the things an agency and a copywriter can do terribly wrong.

Fuller & Smith & Ross

TOWARD the end of my drudgery at NCK, I began hearing rumblings of a creative revolution of a more sophisticated, more honest, less gimmicky kind of work at places like Doyle, Dane, Bernbach, and Papert, Koenig, Lois. I saw ads out there that had humanity and actual wit.

There was hope. I sent my portfolio to several agencies of this new genre and quickly got rejected. How on earth had I expected to get a job at the hottest, most creative agencies in town with a portfolio littered with cliché mediocrity?

Maybe I was a little brainwashed, too. Or my desire to create excellence blinded me to the lack of excellence in the work I had done thus far. After the rejections, I lowered my sights. I realized that I had to take several smaller steps to even be considered for a job in advertising paradise.

I heard there was a Pittsburgh-based agency, Fuller & Smith & Ross (FSR), that had just opened in New York, and was looking to take the town by storm. They had lots of money, and dozens of blue-chip, Midwestern clients and were hiring very bright, young talented creatives. If these guys could work there, why not me? Maybe that was my next step. I wrangled an interview and they hired me.

My instinct had been right. I had some packaged goods work from a big- name New York agency and they needed someone with big-time packaged goods experience. I had filled my book with all the speculative, pretty good, creative work that had never been sold, but what sold FSR about me was the packaged goods crap. No matter the reason, I was on the next rung!

The first week I was there, the agency held a first-year anniversary party at the Top of the Sixes, the chic penthouse bar at 666 Fifth Avenue, the building that housed FSR. It was my first real look at the glamorous side of the ad biz. I'd never seen anything like this — views overlooking all of Manhattan and a room swimming with tuxedoed waiters serving food the likes of which I'd never seen before: little triangular, crustless white bread sandwiches filled with nothing. I'd never seen a finger sandwich or a canapé before and wondered why people bothered to eat them. A nothing sandwich. I realized right then and there that I was in alien, Protestant territory. Not a pig-in-a-blanket in sight. The only pigs I saw were in suits hitting on the sweet, young assistants at the bar.

At the party, I eagerly met a bunch of my new, creative, co-workers. They were young and determined, very much like me. Jerry Dellafemina became a household name in the biz. Evan Stark went on to DDB to create truly legendary work for Alka-Seltzer and Volkswagen. Gene Tashoff and Nat Russo produced quality ads. Dick Cusack, who besides being father of Joan and John Cusack of acting fame, wrote brilliant plays in the evening and mindless drug commercials by day. These were mostly Jews and Italians with a handful of Irish from the boroughs. They had dreams of creating great ads just like I did. I'd finally found a community. All that stood in our way were all the Ivy League stiffs hired to sell the work.

And, indeed, in the time I was there, the agency sold very little of the work we did. This was a Pittsburgh agency with a timid, bow-tie demeanor being asked to sell funny and irreverent work written by New Yorkers to timid, bow-tie clients from Iowa. Hell — I mean — golly, this wasn't easy.

When the clients graciously declined to buy the work, the account guys folded their tents and fell back to the 21 Club around the corner for drinks. They simply didn't have the stomach to fight. Though, they did have the stomach for martinis. Arguing to sell work was ugly, demeaning, and dangerous for your career. Getting sloshed was fun.

These guys could put it away, too. There were a whole group of them who'd go out to 21 with the clients every day at 12:30 p.m., and never come back to work that day. (Frankly, they were lucky to make it to their train to Connecticut.) The next day they could be seen dragging themselves into the office, red-eyed at 10:00 a.m., but by 12:30 p.m. they were once again bright-eyed on their way to their table at 21. (It was no accident that the FSR offices were around the corner from the 21 Club.)

How did the account guys get anything done, you ask? They believed their primary job was to keep the client happy. If the client was happy, then no one was complaining. The idea that someone had to create and produce good advertising and then sell it, thus improving the client's bottom line and attracting new customers, was not their concern. That was long-term thinking. Short-term thoughts were focused on the big mortgage on the Greenwich house that arrived the first of every month.

I recall our creative director, Jack Standish, a pipe-smoking academic from University of Wisconsin, trying to cajole the creative staff into writing ads that might be less difficult to sell.

""Look," he'd say, "it isn't like I want you to sell out. Can't you just give the clients something they can buy — an ad that that doesn't make them feel like they're putting their jobs in jeopardy? Is that so hard?"

For us, this wasn't hard, it was impossible. And damn it, Jack couldn't make us do it. If the clients wouldn't buy good work, that was Jack's problem. He made the big bucks. In his heart, Jack was an academic. His understanding of the business was far more theoretical than rough and tumble. In our view, we were hired to make a mediocre agency great. The fact that the account guys came back every day from meetings with clients with their tails between their legs and a bag of unsold work wasn't our problem.

"Do you want us to turn out crap, Jack?"

"Er, no, of course not, that's not why we hired you."

In all truth, our principal interest was in creating work that would improve our own portfolios. We also believed that if they could somehow sell this more creative, more challenging work, it was good for the clients and for the agency. We could cite chapter and verse how this client or that dramatically grew as a result of great work. And it was, in fact, true. Clients were beginning to see real success in airing funny, witty, unexpected ads. We could relate countless stories about agencies that rose from industry invisibility to the heights of creative prominence simply by creating a few exceptional campaigns. But in truth, at FSR, we knew the great work we were creating would very rarely see the light of day and was done mostly in our own self-interest.

After a while, in an attempt to limit our damage, the agency instituted a Creative Review Board. It was comprised of 10 middle-aged account guys (not a woman in sight) who met at lunch once a week to put their stamp of disapproval on our creative work before it was *not* presented to clients. Notably, there was not one creative person on the Creative Review Board, not even Jack Standish. The work wasn't always killed — many times it was just maimed beyond recognition. This was a weekly contest to see who could emasculate our work most. George Tiger was the most efficient. He was so good at it, he got to start his own agency.

We soon realized that the trick was to somehow keep the review board from ever seeing our work before we got it in front of the client. We learned to engineer the client's "sudden need" to see advertising two days before the review board met, or for the work to be not quite ready to show on the day of their meeting. Or, if all else failed, simply not show up. That was our version of "the dog ate my homework."

From time to time we were successful in avoiding the review board and created some good work. At the end of the day, the clients didn't buy very much of it and it went un-produced. Not so good for an agency, but even worse for a creative person's career. At a certain point, you can't have a portfolio filled with good, un-produced work. It may be exciting, but everybody knows it's not real. It's like peeing down your leg. It feels nice and warm, but nobody sees it.

On rare occasions, some of my quality work was actually sold.

I vividly recall a small space campaign I wrote for Air France that was so well-liked at the agency, they submitted it to the Copy Show; the most prestigious awards competition for copywriter's work in the country. And those ads — my ads — became a finalist!

In the entire show there were only five finalists in each of five categories — a total of 25 ads out of the thousands of ads and TV commercials selected from all the work submitted from every agency in the country. This was very tiny show and therefore, winning was a very a big deal.

In FSRs history, my ads were the first that had ever been selected as finalists in the Copy Show. There was a big awards banquet at the Waldorf with maybe 500 people in attendance. The agency took a table for 10 and actually invited me. At the table were the CEO, and Jack Standish, and Jack's boss, and Jack's boss's boss, all in black tie. And me, in my first, rented tux.

Finally, in the middle of the dinner, my category came up for presentation...

"And here are the finalists..." They went on to name the agency and client to my table's delight. "And the winner... The winner is — The winner is — We're sorry, but the judges have decided *not* to award a medal in this category."

Sitting there in my ill-fitting tux, I felt naked as a jaybird. In the judges' estimation, my work was not worthy of a medal. In fact, the whole category was not worthy. In front of my boss, and my boss's boss, and my boss's boss's boss.

I've won and lost in many subsequent advertising contests, but no loss was anywhere near as humiliating as this. Yet, somehow, the others at the table weren't unhappy at all. They heard the agency name announced at the New York premier advertising event in front of hundreds of the industry's biggest executives and clients for the first time. It was a big win for them. It was a devastating loss for me. I knew I couldn't stay at an agency whose best work wasn't worthy of recognition.

As I said, I created a lot of good work at FSR, but because they couldn't sell it, it remained un-produced.

One of the few exceptions was the work I created in my short stint for Helena Rubenstein. Or I should say, Mme. Rubenstein. Helena Rubenstein was one of the most important women in the history of the cosmetic industry. She, and Estee Lauder, dominated the day, each trying to best the other.

The fact is, "the Madame," as we called her, was getting on in her years when I met her, so this will be a very short story.

The madame didn't get out much those days, so I had to present the ads I'd created to her while she was in bed. Her gorgeous bedroom was in a gorgeous apartment in a gorgeous building on Fifth Avenue overlooking the most gorgeous part of Central Park. If the cocktail party at the Top of the Sixes was the first genuine cocktail party I'd ever been to, this was the first apartment of someone with real wealth I'd ever set foot in. I was fascinated by a Renoir over the bedroom fireplace. I had never seen a Renoir outside the Metropolitan Museum, no less in someone's bedroom. One day, I summoned the courage to stray off the subject of her ads to ask her about it.

"Mme. Rubenstein, what can you tell me about the Renoir over the fireplace?" I asked.

"Which? Oh, that, David. Let me think. Oh, Yes, that's $280,000."

Clearly, she was a major art connoisseur.

At FSR, I had written the kind of ads I had hoped to, but I had no television spots to put on my reel. Aside from a couple pieces for Air France and Rubenstein, and a few banking ads, there wasn't much to show for my time. My real achievements were several dozen exciting ads that had never been sold or had been presented at business meetings for prospective accounts that we never won. (I remember a wonderful campaign for Stokely's Pork and Beans introducing Beanie Weenies. Imagine an adult admitting to writing ads for Beanie Weenies.) But at least this work, unproduced as it was, would begin to represent the talent I thought I had.

With a portfolio of ads tucked under my arm, I set out once again for the new creative world I dreamed was waiting for me.

Before I get onto the next chapter in my creative life, I should tell you something about the career of an advertising creative person.

I can't offer this up any more strongly.

Very simply, the creative work you produce is what gives *you* value. Nothing else matters. If you're a good presenter of your work, that's fine. If you make good relationships with clients, even better. But the quality your work is what establishes your career. It is what gives you job security. It is what makes you desirable to other agencies, and as such, it's what makes you money.

Of course, people leave jobs for money. But for advertising creative people, that has always been the single, greatest mistake. You can make good money from good agencies by doing great work. But, as I said earlier, you can also be paid much more to work at a mediocre agency to create the forgettable. If you go down that road, your career will be forgettable, too.

To put it another way: if you have a good portfolio, you bring the promise of future great work with you. ("What I did for others, I can do for you.") If you take the money and go somewhere like FSR, the agency rarely cashes in on it. If you stay there long enough, the great work you once did gets old and forgotten, and your career slowly dies. Ironically, in time, you even cease to have value at the mediocre agency you are working for. You did the crap for them and after a while, they hold it against you.

"Whatever came of that promising writer named David?"

"He did that crap for *us*?"

I realized, as most ultimately successful creative people did, that the only intelligent reason to leave a job was for one with greater creative opportunity. And in leaving FSR, that's what I was doing.

My Career
Takes a Turn

Carl Ally

WHILE I was at FSR, I had begun to see ads coming out of an agency by the name of Carl Ally, Inc. It was a tiny shop with about three dozen employees, but with a roster of good client names, and even better ads. In the mid-sixties, everywhere I looked, it seemed I saw Carl Ally work.

One day I opened a *Life Magazine* and saw an ad for Volvo with a photo of a dog lifting his leg on the car's tire, the headline — "You can hurt a Volvo, but you can't hurt it much."

I saw an ad for Vespa motor scooter, "Maybe your second car shouldn't be a car."

I saw a commercial that begins with a rush of motorcycles pulling up at a diner at night, shot in the 1950s-style film noir. The cyclists take off their helmets to reveal very old, white-haired women who proceed to go into the diner and order tea. As they sip their tea, the announcer says, "And you thought tea was for weak, little-old ladies." To take the dated perception of tea and stand it on its head was brilliant.

All these ads and commercials were from Carl Ally, Inc. This was an agency I would kill to work for.

Before I relate my introduction to Ally, the agency, I should introduce you to Carl Ally, the man.

Carl was a larger-than-life salesman, a mesmerizing speaker, and a genuinely crazy person. He was, without question, one of the smartest and most courageous people I ever met — and perhaps the most self-destructive.

In the early 1960s, the model for an advertising agency CEO was: a handsome fellow of high White Anglo-Saxon Protestant (WASP) lineage, born to a prominent old family, graduated from one of the Ivies, had maybe a Harvard or Yale BA, and perhaps a Wharton MBA His family was well-connected with the rich and powerful. This was important because accounts were often won by family associations and country club pals, not by the quality of the work an agency produced.

Carl's life and background was the antithesis of this model. He had no powerful friends and no family connections. At an earlier moment, no doors would have opened for Carl. He was of the wrong ethnicity with the wrong upbringing. He grew up in Detroit, the son of immigrant parents—his father Turkish, his mother Italian.

Carl joined the U.S. Air Force in World War II, re-upped for the Korean War and became an ace fighter pilot. When he returned to civilian life, he enrolled at the University of Michigan on the GI Bill. There, he majored in English, earned a master's degree, and subsequently taught the subject. He soon realized he was far too ambitious for the academic life and entered the marketing industry. He first joined General Electric (GE) in Ohio and then went to Campbell-Ewald, an advertising agency that specialized in auto advertising in Detroit.

Carl worked in Detroit for several years, moved to work at their New York City office, but soon left. In Carl's obituary, it says he was fired from there because he thought he was smarter than his bosses. That sounds about right—that he thought he was, and that he actually was, smarter.

He used his car experience to land a job at Papert Koenig Lois (PKL), which was one of the most creative agencies in the country. While he was working on a Peugeot campaign, a former client who was now at Volvo, approached Carl. He asked if PKL would give up the Peugeot business to take on this newcomer to the American market. Carl was very much in favor of this. It would make him pivotal to what could be a very lucrative account and thus, make him much more valuable to the agency. Carl approached PKL management to propose this offer. Not unexpectedly, they said they certainly would not. Why would they give up Peugeot, an established account, for an upstart competitor from Scandinavia?

At this point, less ambitious men would have folded their tents and gone back to work. Not Carl. The wheels in his head were turning.

He approached Volvo with another proposition:

"Unfortunately, PKL doesn't want you. But I've got a better opportunity for you. Why don't you let me personally build an agency around you? You and Volvo will be its star account!"

He actually had the balls to ask! Ninety-nine out of 100 companies would say: "What are you, nuts? We're supposed to put our new-to-America account into an agency that doesn't exist?"

Somehow Volvo, in a moment of utter impetuousness or exceptional prescience, agreed to Carl's outrageous idea. Why? Because Carl was a remarkable salesman.

Thus, with one account and next to nothing in the bank, Carl opened the doors of Carl Ally, Inc. To say he was a risk-taker would be inaccurate. Even when he had a lot to lose, I never knew Carl to be aware of risk. I was told he was the same way as a former wartime fighter pilot. In later years, stories circulated that Carl was the inspiration for Yosarian, the hero in Joseph Heller's *Catch-22*. True? You'd have to ask Joe Heller. But it made sense to a lot of us.

Carl had a framed quotation in his office, "COMFORT THE AFFLICTED, AFFLICT THE COMFORTABLE." The saying was written by the famous, early 20th century, muck-raking, Chicago journalist, F. P. Dunne. It was later appropriated by an even more famous character, the labor organizer, Mother Jones. Mother Jones was once dubbed the most dangerous woman in America — and I guess Carl yearned for that title, too. (Not the woman part.)

Now, it's one thing to want to "comfort the afflicted," but to follow the dictum "afflict the comfortable" as head of an advertising agency that's trying to make a living by pursuing comfortable companies as clients is clearly fool hardy. But that was Carl. He was a born socialist playing in the ultimate capitalist's game.

Carl was also not the prince of style. He could wear a $1000 suit and make it look like it came from the bottom corner of a closet. I rarely saw him when his shirttails weren't hanging from his pants. I'm not sure whether this was because he was sticking it in the eye of the impeccable, pin-striped suit clients, or he was just a mess. One day he showed up at a posh country club to meet a client for golf — not in a Ralph Lauren Polo shirt — but in a tank top known as a "wife beater". Was it because he didn't know better? No. He knew better.

When this anti-establishment businessman opened his agency's doors, he partnered with two remarkable people he had worked with in Detroit to run the creative side of the agency — Jim Durfee and Amil Gargano. Both had followed Carl to the New York office of Campbell Ewald. Eventually, they each went their separate ways; Carl to Papert Koenig Lois, Jim to J. Walter Thompson (JWT) as a writer, and Amil to Benton and Bowles as an art director.

Jim was a huge man, 6'4" with shoulders as wide as Madison Avenue. He'd been a tackle on the Western Michigan University football team, but he wrote like Dylan Thomas. These were the days when print ads often contained long and intelligent copy and Jim's was among the most brilliant. Much of what I know about writing copy I learned from Jim and from Ed McCabe (who you'll hear about shortly.)

Amil Gargano, Jim's creative partner, was every bit as brilliant, perhaps more so. The son of first-generation Italian parents, Amil wanted to be a serious artist and had gone to Cranbrook Academy, one of the greatest Art and Design schools in the country. It was the mid-west version of Cooper Union; only the best of the best got in. At Cranbrook, one of Amil's teachers opened his eyes to advertising and the rest is history.

For Jim and Amil, there was not much opportunity in those days to do breakthrough creative work at J. Walker Thompson (JWT) or B&B, so they slogged along until the call came from Carl. The new agency, Carl Ally, Inc., opened its doors, and soon Amil and Jim began to create the work they had long dreamed of.

Like so many creative people working at uninspired and uninspiring agencies, I followed the work being created at Ally and at Doyle Dane Bernbach and at Papert Koenig Lois, and Jack Tinker & Partners with intense interest. These agencies were my Valhalla. There were fewer than a handful of them in the entire industry. To starry-eyed creatives, the people who worked there were gods.

Three years after Carl Ally opened, I was focused on the idea of joining this brilliant creative band. I was hoping to finally enter the creative major leagues. But frankly, I barely had the credentials.

If you came from mediocre agencies, as I did, the bulk of what made it into magazines or onto TV was creatively worthless. Showing terrible work in your portfolio proved that you had experience—the bad experience of creating them and the bad judgment in having them represent your creativity.

What was I to do? I could say I was a copywriter but, in the 2½ years I'd been a writer, I could show little produced work that I was proud of.

I had created few quality ads that were actually produced, so the work I offered in my portfolio was ninety percent speculative. These were ads that had been presented to clients but never bought, or shown at new business presentations to potential clients, but never bought. The common denominator—never bought. My portfolio was not a reflection of work I had produced, but the work I had hoped to produce.

I recall years later, when I was a creative head at Carl Ally, looking at the portfolio of a young copywriter. His ads were really good. Several started to look very familiar. It suddenly dawned on me that these were ads that friends of mine had created. Didn't Roy Grace do this? I know that ad. That's Evan Stark's. As I continued to flip through the book, I suddenly came upon two ads I had written.

"Boy, this guy's got balls," I thought. Didn't he realize that in our little corner of the agency world we all were familiar with each other's work? But I played along and kept flipping through. Finally, I very quietly looked up and matter-of-factly said, "Good book! You created all these ads?" His eyes opened wide, he suddenly knew the jig was up. "Err... Oh, no. These aren't ads I've written. No... These are ads I would *like* to write."

I'm sure lots of portfolios had an occasional ad that was appropriated from another writer. Sometimes, people take credit for something they didn't create because they were in the room when it was created. But this kind of wanton theft was something rare. In those days, if a great ad appeared in a magazine, it was instantly known across the creative community. We didn't need the internet to make things go viral.

I wish I could say that I was able to warn my creative cohorts of this portfolio of pilfered work, but who knew where he and his collection of other people's property would show up. Alas, they wouldn't know enough to call me. How were they to know he'd visited me. I can only hope that he was more successful writing ads than stealing them.

But back to me... The most I can say for myself when I was peddling my portfolio is that I knew the difference between good and bad ads. And at least they were *my* ads.

So, I was working at FSR, and with portfolio in hand, I applied to Carl Ally, Inc.

The process of applying at any agency was painful, but Ally's was worse. You dropped off your portfolio along with a cover letter and then waited... And waited some more. After about a month, I believed that my portfolio had been lost. But out of the blue, I received a call from Ed McCabe's secretary.

Ed was third in command, creatively, after Jim and Amil. The work Ed had created at the agency was nothing short of brilliant. Some of it was what brought the agency to my attention in the first place.

If getting into Ally to see McCabe was heaven, actually sitting in front of Ed and showing him my portfolio was sheer hell. This was the first real, creative opportunity I had in my young career. This was not another job. This was *the* job. The first I ever lusted after.

Would Ed hate my portfolio? Would he say "Is that all you have — spec work?" I held my breath. Ed interrogated me for what felt like hours. He asked questions about every single ad. "What was your motivation for this headline?" "Why did you start the copy this way?" If he had hated the ads, the entire trajectory of my career would have changed. Ultimately, I would have likely fallen victim to the big money of mediocre agencies and never had a chance to see the promised land.

But Ed liked my book! To this day, I have no idea what he liked or why. But he liked it enough to send me and my book on to Jim and Amil. Jim and Amil liked it, too. Unbelievable! AND they made me an offer.

It was an offer that any husband and father of two young boys could not possibly take.

At the time, for all the crappy work I was doing at FSR, I was making $35,000 a year, which in those days was pretty big money. (You could buy a house in Scarsdale for $60,000.)

Amil and Jim told me I was hired at $22,000. Huh?

Yes, they offered me a $13,000 cut in salary. They said that's all they could afford. I'm not sure that's true, but I came to realize that they wanted you to appreciate the enormous opportunity you were being given — in blood.

I didn't hesitate. I took the job with its $13,000 step backwards on the spot. Was I crazy? Yes, I guess I was, but in the same way Carl was crazy for starting an agency without two nickels to rub together.

As I said earlier, I believed — and will believe 'til my last day — that the work you produce is everything. It is the ticket to a higher salary, to job security, and most important, to going home at night proud of what you do. Who knew whether an offer from one of the agencies I idolized would ever come again? I knew the pay cut was worth it.

I went home that night and told my wife about the offer and the giant cut in salary. She didn't give me a hard time.

I've never really thought about that until this moment. She might have responded the way many wives who were concerned with their family's financial security would. She could have questioned my sanity. She could have felt financially abandoned. And she would have had every right. I already had two small children and a mortgage. But she believed in me, and she believed in my dream.

After decades of being divorced and a lifetime of "too late," I'd like to say "Thank you."

By the way, my instinct about taking the Ally offer without hesitation was a good one. About six months after I was hired, Amil made an offer to an art director. When asked if he could have the weekend to think it over, Amil told him:

"If you have to think about it, you don't want us enough. Forget we made the offer."

Ally wanted your loyalty and deep-felt appreciation for the career-changing opportunity you were being given or it was no deal.

Once I got to Ally, it was not quite a picnic. I was working for Ed McCabe. Ed was one of the most demanding people ever to walk the creative corridors. Some said he actually liked abusing those who worked for him. To be clear, I'm not completely sure he enjoyed berating his underlings, I think he saw it as part of his persona. Ed did not simply attack your work, he attacked you! More than a few folks left his office in tears. About two years after

I started working for Ed, he actually wrote a slogan for himself: "Learn by being crushed."

Maybe I was a quick learner, or maybe I didn't take well to being crushed, but Ed saw that I couldn't be easily broken. After a while, he eased up on me a bit. Aside from the berating, Ed was a great teacher. I attribute to Ed and Jim Durfee, who was always the spirit of gentleness, my ability to understand compelling ideas, to write humorously and convincingly, and to think out of the box. To them, and perhaps most to my creative partner in later years at Carl Ally, Inc., Amil Gargano, who taught me to think conceptually, I owe my career.

Ed left Carl Ally about two years after I started to open Scali, McCabe and Sloves (SMS.) It was an agency created in the spirit of Carl Ally and Papert Koenig Lois. (No surprise as this is where the three SMS partners had come from.) Ed went on to create a score of memorable ads and commercials. Among many other successes, Ed put Purdue Chicken on the map, He turned Frank Purdue into the star of commercials with the theme: "It takes a tough man make a tender chicken." He created the Hebrew National campaign, "We answer to a higher authority." He inherited the Volvo business from Ally and did great work. And, to his embarrassment, he wrote a series of commercials starring O.J. Simpson for Hertz. (Even the greats are not always great.)

I worked with a number of legendary art directors at Ally. My first creative partner (he was hired the same day as I) is without question the most uniquely creative person I've known: Ron Barrett. Ron saw the world differently than most advertising folks do. His imagination and his sense of humor was simply one-of-a-kind. Ron was also a remarkable illustrator. No surprise that after several years in advertising, he gave up the frustration and compromise and became a creator of children's books. Many became classics and some became movies. No doubt you and your children have read or seen *Cloudy with a Chance of Meatballs*.

I subsequently teamed up with three art directors who are all now in the Advertising Creative Hall of Fame: Ralph Ammirati, who went on to begin his own agency, Ammirati Puris. Roy Grace, who went on to start his own agency, Grace & Rothschild. And, of course, Amil Gargano. How lucky can you be to team with four of the most legendary art directors of their time?

***

Before I continue on with my journey at this ground-breaking agency, it would be good to put Carl Ally, Inc. in more context.

Many books have been written on the history of advertising, but for purposes of this less scholarly memoir, I'll just give you a quick outline.

From the beginning of modern advertising, around the turn of the 20th century, ads had been very much product driven. The advertiser attempted to sell things by reason of a product's demonstrable superiority to its competitors.

As an example, in the 1950s, David Ogilvy wrote one of the most famous headlines in the history of automotive advertising: "At 60 miles an hour, the loudest noise in this new Rolls Royce comes from the electric clock." He took a small product fact—I don't know that it was actually true—and made it representative of the craftsmanship and luxury of the Rolls.

Also in the 1950s, Rosser Reeves, another early force in advertising at Ted Bates & Co., attempted of codify his agency's product-centric approach with something he called a "Unique Selling Proposition" or USP. It became the mantra for the agency.

For each of Bates & Co.'s clients, they attempted to create a memorable set of words that would give the reader or viewer a rational reason to believe that this product was demonstratively better than all its competitors. The USP was supposed to be one that the product could forever own. I'll give you a few of Reeves' slogans to give you an idea of a USP:

"Wonder Bread builds strong bodies 8 ways."

For Certs: "It's a candy mint. It's a breath mint. It's two… two… two mints in one."

For M&Ms: "It melts in your mouth, not in your hands."

The headlines may seem arcane today, but they are indicative of what drove advertising then. And since they were repeated ad nauseam over the years, they stuck.

At that time, the idea of a rational sell—the assumption that people buy things with their heads and not their hearts—was the most widely held and successful way to reach the consumer. This singular product-driven fact was repeated in every commercial, in every jingle. There was almost no attempt at humor or any real humanity.

But a monumental advertising change began to take place in the late 1950s with the emergence of Doyle Dane Bernbach.

If there is any one person who can be credited with the change that brought advertising into today's world, it is William Bernbach.

In 1949, Bernbach was working for one of the most successful Jewish-run agencies in New York, Grey Advertising. Bill was then working on a campaign for Ohrbach's, one of New York's leading fashion retailers. At a certain point, the Ohrbach's folks approached Bill and asked whether he would open his own agency with them as their first client. Ohrbach's was so committed to Bernbach, they offered to pay all the agency's bills until it got on its feet. Unheard of.

Doyle Dane Bernbach was off and running. The first Ohrbach's ads were like nothing the advertising business had seen before: witty, chic, and contemporary. In 1964, Bernbach remarked about his work on Ohrbach's: "A store must have a personality or character. If it doesn't, it's nothing."

On the shoulders of Ohrbach's, Volkswagen brought its business to the agency. Volkswagen ads like "Lemon" — the first ad that seemed to put down the advertiser — appeared, followed by one of the most famous slogans ever written: "Think Small." The agency took off. Avis, Polaroid, Jamaica (the country), American Airlines and many more signed on.

DDB changed advertising forever.

Of everything Bernbach said and wrote, of which there are several books written, one quote articulates how profoundly his agency changed the idea of advertising:

"Nothing is so powerful as an insight into human nature."

If Reeves began with product attributes, Bernbach began with our individual and collective humanity. The basis of Bernbach's advertising was its ability to understand who we are as people. He used this awareness to illuminate the relationship between us and the product he was selling to us.

DDB created ads and commercials that were grounded in wit, in self-deprecation, and in real emotion. People in their commercials spoke the way real people speak, situations weren't contrived, and headlines had genuine charm. It was as if a light bulb had suddenly illuminated the industry.

In truth, the light bulb didn't illuminate every aspect of the business until many years later. (And in some cases, it still hasn't.) The big, packaged goods agencies continued to create the same old same old. Even today, you still see TV commercials that are hardly different than they were fifty years ago. But change did come to a portion of the business. Bill Bernbach gave birth to an army of agency acolytes — Jack Tinker, Mary Wells, Julian Koenig, George Lois, Shep Kurnit, Carl Ally.

Each started their agencies with Bernbach's new creative insight. And over time, each gave birth to a new generation of agencies carrying on this tradition. In New York, Ammirati Puris, Scali McCabe, Grace & Rothschild, and I'm proud to say, Altschiller Reitzfeld emerged. We, and dozens of unnamed agencies across the country are all indebted to Bernbach's brilliance. Remarkably, since he gave us this new way of speaking to the audience some fifty years ago, nothing of note has come along to change it. The media has changed, the advertising formats have been modified, the internet has had a profound effect, but there has not been a truly new way of harnessing the relationship between the consumable and the consumer.

Beginning with DDB, a new level of graphic design emerged. Bob Gage and Helmut Crone at DDB, Amil and Ralph Ammirati at Ally were at the forefront at the agencies. At graphic design and type design houses people like Paul Rand, Massimo Vignelli, and Herb Lubalin were gaining fame. Copy was crafted on the page word by word. Type was cut apart by hand, letter by letter. World-class editorial photographers were hired to shoot ads — Irving Penn, Gordon Parks, Richard Avedon, Bert Stern. Copywriters were actually writers. Long, articulate copy was the order of the day. Copy painted pictures, told stories, carefully articulated arguments.

***

In the early 1960s, *Life Magazine* was the darling of the media business.

Even if clients didn't have the budget for it, Carl pushed them to kick off their campaigns with a spread in *Life Magazine*. He insisted it would give them instant visibility. What he left out was that a big splashy ad in *Life* would give his agency instant recognition.

At this same time, television advertising was in its infancy. A few years earlier, there were only live commercials. Betty Furness stood in front of her refrigerator. Ronald Reagan touted GE. Commercials were little more than talking heads.

Out of the blue, commercials began to be filmed rather than aired live and presented the kind of drama found in movies. The industry responded with engaging commercials unlike anything seen on TV before.

Still photographers became the first commercial directors. "People photographers" like Howard Zieff and Steve Horn were not only creating evocative ads (See Levy's Rye Bread), they were creating brilliantly humorous, touching, and *human* commercials.

Over the life of Carl Ally, Inc., many truly famous campaigns were created: FedEx, Volvo, Pan Am, Fiat, Hertz, Tonka Toys, Cinzano, Saab, MCI, Barney's. I was lucky enough to have written some of them. There were many companies that Ally built from scratch and turned into behemoths. (Ally was Fred Smith's and FedEx's first agency.) Yet, one after the other, no matter how great each client's successes, Ally lost all of them.

How does that happen? How can you create monumental success for a company and then lose their business? There are lots of ways, but Carl was a master at two:

1. You make the client uncomfortable with the advertising process.
2. You exclude the client from sharing credit when it achieves success.

As I said earlier, it's never smart make the clients feel that they've gone out on a limb. You want to make them feel that, in pursuing a certain direction, there's no danger to their company or, more importantly, to their careers.

Many agencies have learned to use research to make this kind of decision-making appear less risky. This may lead you to believe that research guarantees success; far from it. The most important thing research does is take the client personally off the hook. If a new product or a new commercial should fail, the client can blame the research that supported the effort.

"It wasn't me. It was research that gave the project the green light. I'm a marketing professional. I merely responded to the evidence."

Even though research made a client comfortable, Ally resisted it. The man and the agency fought against it every step of the way. The agency, and I think rightly, believed that research can tell you what was, not what will be. In focus groups, people cannot be counted on to champion new thinking. In public, the agency contended, individuals attending focus groups would not necessarily tell you what they really felt, but what they thought was acceptable to say. Given this, the deck was always stacked against commercials articulating things in a new way or promoting new ideas. Research, to Carl Ally, Inc., was the enemy of innovation.

At Ally, the client was driven to buy commercials on faith without the crutch of, or even contrary to, the conclusions of research. For many, this meant that the ground was always shaky beneath them. Some clients felt that they were sharing a great advertising adventure into unchartered waters; it was exciting. But for the faint of heart, for those who worried that their first mistake in approving commercials would be their last, this meant there was no place to hide.

For this reason, Ally was most alluring to the founders or CEOs of companies. This was a group whose entrepreneurial DNA was akin to Carl's. These CEOs were not looking over their shoulders wondering what the boss would think — they were the boss.

To clients like these, Carl would boast that they were changing the world. The idea of "changing the world" was one of Carl's favorite sales tools and his ideal corporate platform. What could be more seductive and ego-gratifying to an entrepreneur?

"You are a visionary, my friend. *You* are changing the world, and we are simply informing the world about it."

The grand positionings for his clients were remarkably consistent in this regard.

FedEx was, "changing the way the world does business." Pan Am, "opened the world to air travel." Fiat touted, "the small car is the future of automobiles." Volvo, "brought the world a new level of automotive safety." And IBM declared, "Machines should work. People should think."

If you'll allow me to indulge in some nickel and dime psychology, Carl would never accept that what he did for a living was simply hawking goods. His goal was to have a real and lasting impact on anything he touched. Through his clients, and his vision of his client's exploits, he could achieve that.

Certainly, Carl wanted to be rich. (I remember Carl announcing the winning of an account to a handful of us. "I'm gonna be rich," he roared. "I mean... *we're* gonna be rich.") But even more than wealth, Carl wanted to change the world and be famous for it. It should come as no surprise that his great, unrealized ambition was to be Ambassador to the United Nations.

Not all clients who came to Ally, however, were in a position to change the world. Some were simply battling against far more rich and powerful competitors. These clients needed to break out from the back of the pack; to do something truly ground-breaking. For them, Ally was a perfect fit. These clients were not worried about down-side risk. They were already living on the downside. They needed a marketing home run, not a single. And Ally was noted for home runs.

To this group, Carl's approach was mesmerizing—"You're in trouble and we are the doctor. We're going to save you." Even though the agency asked these clients to take enormous leaps of faith, what did they have to lose? They were in trouble already.

But as one might expect, shortly after these clients reached some modicum of success, they would leave the agency. They no longer had to endure what they now saw as risk-taking. They no longer had to subordinate themselves to Carl's bullying.

We've discussed client discomfort as a reason for leaving. We should also talk about the other reason for their departure: Carl's utter unwillingness to share credit for success.

One thing that I learned early in my career was to allow the clients to feel that it was only through their insight, or courage, or perseverance, or something or other, that success was achieved.

In short, if you thought about the long term, you'd deflect credit to client. And in some ways, this was appropriate. After all, without a client, your work would never be anything more than speculative. But more importantly, you share credit because a client needs it, too. Like anyone, he has to go home to his family and tell them what brilliant thing he has done, what great contribution he has made. There's no glory in telling the wife, "You should have seen how brilliant the agency was today. Without them, I wouldn't have had a clue."

The client ego needs to take ownership, too. If a client risks his job in the battle, he has the right to share in the victory.

Ally would never allow this. In Carl's mind, the agency was the home of marketing intelligence. To him, that's why clients needed agencies. Clients, he felt, were mostly brilliant in creating products and then recognizing their agency-dependency in marketing them. Sometimes, Carl's self-aggrandizement was subtle and sometimes, it was breathtakingly boorish.

There are many examples, but one incident, I think, may be enough.

One day we were presenting a print campaign to the marketing head of Pan Am. Carl made the introductory remarks and we proceeded to take the client through about a dozen magazine ads. They were really good ads.

Immediately after we finished presenting, the gracious Pan Am exec. didn't hesitate to give praise. "This is really an exceptional campaign. There's not one ad I wouldn't run. In fact, why doesn't the agency choose the order you wish to run them in and let's get started."

I had never heard anything like this. The client was not only approving every ad in the entire campaign — on the spot — he ceded all the power in determining the order that the work would be run.

Several of us were about to thank him for his trust, but before we got a chance, Carl interjected, "You're right, the ads are brilliant. And now I'm going to tell you why."

I saw the client's demeanor change. In the moment of his great generosity, he had been denied to chance to be gracious. He had been robbed of the opportunity of bestowing his blessing. It was the first step toward losing the business, which we ultimately did.

Pan Am

If you're in the business of writing commercials, sooner or later you get to work with celebrities.

In fact, part of the glamour of the advertising business comes with the promise of working with A-listers. What most people don't realize is that with the glamour of celebrity comes the promise of pain. While some can be charming, more often than not, celebrities and the minions that surround them can be the most exasperating people on earth.

While working on Pan Am with Amil, we created a campaign that relied on celebrities. It was one of the best—and worst—experiences of my career.

Pan Am, from the beginning of passenger air travel, had been known as America's premier flag carrier, and certainly, they should have been. Juan Tripp, the founder of Pan Am, had opened up the world to air travel.

For years, they boasted the slogan, "The world's most experienced airline," and they were. But Pan Am's preeminent reputation in the industry was beginning to wane.

Amil and I felt we needed to give new meaning to the aging slogan. As we thought about the idea of "the world 's most experienced," we asked ourselves what makes all that experience relevant to the passenger? What's in it for them?

To us, all this experience implied something more than know-how. It ultimately suggested a greater sense of safety. This led us to consider something that had never been discussed publicly in the airline business before, but to us, was very much on the minds of anyone who has ever flown: fear.

There you are at 30,000 feet, you can't see the ground, the plane begins to bounce around and half the passengers go white-knuckled. It's not even rough enough for barf bags, but people are beginning to mentally put their lives in order. *"Do I still want to leave my mom's ruby ring to my niece? Have we ever discussed who should officiate at our funeral? Are we current with payments for the burial plots?*

Everybody — deep-down — understands that flying is unnatural for humans. If we were meant to fly, we'd have feathers and a tail. Certainly, no one had ever dared to discuss this fear in an airline commercial.

There are all sorts of issues that are never discussed in commercials even though they are an elephant in the room. Advertisers worry that bringing them up would suddenly cause a dark secret to be revealed — as if it were ever a secret. They've concluded that, as long as people don't discuss these things openly, these things don't exist.

The basis of some of the best comedy is saying what one dare not. Comedy understands that saying the things that resonate in everyone's psyche can be profoundly powerful, and often so uncomfortable that they become funny.

But to advertisers, truth, like flying, is scary.

Nonetheless, in the face of all this denial, we presented the fear of flying idea to Pan Am. To their credit, and somewhat to our surprise, they bought it. They recognized the truth of it and the public relations value in bringing to light something that had never been publicly discussed.

Sadly, agencies rarely acknowledge the debt they owe to their clients for having the courage to allow the truly ground-breaking work to come to market. (And the best work — the most highly creative work — is often the riskiest work.) The clients at Pan Am did not shrink from the risk. So now, years after the fact, I thank them.

Now came the execution of this very troubling subject.

It appeared to us that it would be quite powerful to feature "white-knucklers" who were willing to discuss their fear. But rather than using regular folks, who you'd expect to be nervous, we'd use people who you wouldn't expect: larger than life stars who fly a lot. They fly so much that you'd never imagine they'd be afraid.

At this point in advertising history, many celebrities were still dubious of appearing in commercials. It was thought of as "selling out." The universe of willing stars was rather small compared to today, but we compounded our problem. We also wanted these celebrities to be virgins to commercials. We looked for stars who were famous but had not yet been exposed that way.

As we canvassed agents for names, we found all the usual suspects: stars who had long ago ceased to twinkle and actors who fell into the "Oh, I know that guy… it's… it's… his name is on the tip of my tongue"- category.

But we found several bona fide stars, truly big names who were willing: David Niven, Joan Crawford, and Bill Cosby. (Well, Joan Crawford may have been attempting to re-start a career, but what a career!)

By the way, we negotiated with the celebrities by creating what's called a "favored-nations clause." That is, offering the same salary to all. This would keep us from needing to negotiate with each one, or worse, playing their agent's against one another.

David Niven

THE first celebrity we filmed was David Niven. He was a dream.

A little background: Niven had been educated at the Royal Military Academy Sandhurst and served as a lieutenant in the Black Watch, the Royal Regiment of Scotland, before coming to Hollywood. Legend has it, he was brought to America by the heiress, Doris Duke, and given acting opportunities by his Hollywood friends, simply because he was such a charmer. People simply loved having him around. He came to the attention of Samuel Goldwyn and signed with MGM. If Goldman wanted someone charming and debonaire for a film, Niven was his man.

Amil and I flew to London and met with Niven at The Connaught Hotel before the shoot. The Connaught is one of the most venerable institutions in the city. I remember Niven asked us to his suite for a drink. He pressed a buzzer by his chair, and before the buzzer stopped vibrating, a waiter opened the door. The waiter must have had his hand on the door knocker for half an hour waiting for the buzzer to buzz. I've never seen that kind of service. I'm not sure whether this level of response was usual for the hotel or because it was David Niven, but either way I was impressed. I remember, too, that Niven was dressed impeccably; his tie even matched his pocket square. We spoke at length with him and within an hour we were simply gaga. Niven was so charming; he seemed to represent a higher species of human. He was humorous in a sly, understated way. He had a combination of warmth and civility that was breath-taking. (I have never experienced it since.)

By the time we saw him on the set, he had memorized the script and made it his own. As he had done so many times in film, he was always in character, and yet always David Niven. This is what the great movie stars did. Always in character, always themselves. Think Clark Gable, Spencer Tracy, Gregory Peck.

During the commercial, you believed Niven's feelings of discomfort during flight were genuine. Was he truly a white-knuckle flier? Who knows, but he sure acted like one. We had planned for an eight-hour shooting day. After the first few takes, we knew it wouldn't take that long. Niven took direction brilliantly, he mastered every nuance, and each take was better than the last. We ran out of things to ask him to do. We were done in three hours and that was stretching it. So, we went to lunch. We never wanted the day to end. As I reflect back on a long career in advertising, this is one experience I truly treasure.

So often celebrities are a disappointment. You equate the people they play in movies with who they are. Or you believe that their brilliance as musicians parallels their brilliance as people. Or you believe that comedians should be as funny in "real life" as they are one stage. Not so.

Frankly, comedians—as a group—are a morose, insecure bunch. They light up in the spotlight, but often are hell to be with in real life. There are only two I've spent time with who weren't major-league depressive: Mel Brooks and Carl Reiner.

There were no surprises with the Pan Am commercial. Niven's performance was as impeccable in the final product as it was while on set. The campaign was off to a great start.

On to Joan Crawford! God help us.

Joan Crawford

THE experience with Ms. Crawford could not have been more different than the one we had with David Niven.

Before the shoot, she invited us to lunch at her apartment to get to know us. It was a truly odd meeting in a truly odd setting.

She lived in the penthouse apartment of a high rise in the East 70s of Manhattan. This was not at all what we expected. This was not one of the grand, old edifices built early in the century with palatial rooms and breathtaking views. The was a bland, post-war building off Third Avenue. It looked out onto a one-story sandwich shop and watch repair store.

When you walked in the apartment, the first thing you saw, on a small round table just feet from the door, was her Academy Award for Best Actress in *Mildred Pierce*. This wasn't discretely tucked in a bookcase along with the other bric-a-brac. This was on a table, by itself, with a spotlight shining down on it.

The next things you saw were the Keane paintings. Are you familiar with Margaret Keane's paintings? Trust me, you'd remember. They're these bizarre paintings of children with the big, sad eyes. They were everywhere in the apartment. I imagine she had one of the largest collections in the world. They gave me the creeps. Why anyone would surround themself with this circus of sadness is beyond me.

The apartment itself was a pretty standard, Upper East Side space; utterly bland. But the furnishings could have been lifted from Beverly Hills. They were designed by Carlton Varney, the famous Hollywood decorator of the 1940s/1950s. The furniture was all lime green and yellow leather (or maybe leatherette.) I guess she wanted to bring old Hollywood with her to New York. The combination of the apartment décor and the manner of the actress made the experience surreal. She even had napkins embossed with "Joan Crawford." (I pocketed one. After shooting the spot, I blew my nose in it and threw it away.

During lunch, we quickly realized that this commercial shoot was much more important to Ms. Crawford than we thought. While she had been one of the most famous stars in the history of film, she had been out of the public eye for several years now. In her mind, this was to be her big comeback. Remember Gloria Swanson in Sunset Boulevard, "I'm ready for my close-up, Mr. DeMille". This was it — for real!

Had we taken note of her behavior, we would have somehow found a way to get out of the contract before we left the apartment. We suspected the shoot would be treacherous and it was. But we thought: how much damage could an actor do in a day? We were about to find out.

The day of the shoot, within moments of Ms. Crawford's coming out of make-up (which took four hours), she marched up to our director, a lovely and talented guy by the name of Dick Lowe.

"The way I see it, Mr. Director," she said. "I'll begin with my back to the camera and slowly... soooo very slowly, I'll turn around and the audience will see Joan Crawford for the first time."

You could hear the audience in her mind gasp. We were in trouble. Not only was she attempting to direct her own shoot, but she was also referring to herself in the third person.

She demonstrated her idea. The dramatic opening spin lasted 10 seconds. Her idea might work in a two-hour movie, but it would take a full third of the 30-second commercial before she uttered a syllable. We knew we couldn't afford this kind of theatrical indulgence, but we had to allow her to attempt it. After all, *she* had an Oscar and, as she was quick to remind us several times that day, we were just advertising hacks.

For a 30-second commercial when there are actors speaking on camera, I never wrote more than 22 seconds worth of dialogue. This would give the script time to breathe and leave the actors a little room to actually act.

Ms. Crawford's first take on my 22-second script was 56 seconds; more than twice the length of the 30-second spot we needed. Of course, this included the 12 seconds for her silent and exaggerated spin around. Her second take was 54 seconds. She sped up a little more on take three; 52 seconds. Still 22 seconds over.

After half a dozen more extended takes, we persuaded her to give up the spin. We would have edited it out of the shot anyway. It was a self-indulgent gesture, melodramatic to say the least. This was not an easy discussion.

"David," Ms. Crawford imperiously said, (well at least she didn't call me Mr. Writer), "I'm reading as fast as I can, you've written far too many words here."

The fact is, I could write whole commercials into the dramatic pauses she took, but I had to do something to appease her. So, I cut five more seconds out of the script. Her readings now were 40-, 40-, and 37 seconds.

Another six takes, I cut another three seconds. I'm down to 14 seconds of script. We are now begging her to try to read a 30-second commercial in the time it would take a 6-year-old reader to accomplish it.

We go for another take. 34 seconds. The next, 32 seconds. I can't cut any more, there'll be no words left. Finally, after about eight more takes, a reading comes in at exactly 30 seconds. But it is a very strange read, somewhat stilted, with pauses in very unexpected places.

I know that after all these takes, Ms. Crawford is on the ropes. When she signed on, I imagine she expected to do one or two takes and waltz out. After all, this was not *Mildred Pierce*. This was *only* a commercial, her big come-back perhaps, but a commercial, nevertheless.

I rushed over to her, knowing that if she's told the take is within the time frame, she could bolt. "That was terrific, wonderful, Ms. Crawford. But we're about a half-second over," I say. "Let's quickly go for another. We're right there. We'll get it this time." I knew the last take was in time, but it's such a weird reading, we need to try to get another quickly, "Dick, let's roll them."

Suddenly, I hear the script guy from about thirty yards away shout out, "Oh, no, Ms. Crawford, it's right on time."

"Oh, no," is right. Mister Brown Nose has just killed us. As I feared, I hear our beloved star say, "On time? Really. Now, who do I believe about the timing? The script man, whose job it is to time things, or the writer? You've got your take, boys. It's a wrap."

There was no way we could cajole her to go for another take. She'd had enough. When making commercials, you try to get a dozen takes of a scene on time so you have something to select and edit from. In this way, you can edit out the bad parts of otherwise good takes and put them together with other good parts of good takes. We had only one take and no place to cut to. No good and bad, just bad.

When we saw the film at the editor's, we realized our fears were slightly overblown from the sheer ugliness of the experience. The reading was not bad, just very, very odd. Sadly, we had no choice except to put it on the air. The Crawford contract required that if we shot it, we'd run it. Clearly, her lawyers knew who they were dealing with.

When it finally ran, we held our breath. Will people know it's as weird as it is? Not on your life! They thought it was "Soooo Joan Crawford."

"How real."

"How she made the script her own."

"Such drama, such surprising timings.

"*Mildred Pierce* quality."

"Now that's acting!"

We got lucky. The agency had a monumental creative reputation in the business. At that moment in our careers, we could do no wrong. Amazing how when you're known for excellence, people presume excellence.

As my old boss, Carl Ally, once said (after a meeting that should have been a disaster, but turned out OK,) "Another day, undetected."

Bill Cosby

By the time I got through the Joan Crawford spot, I needed a vacation. The Bill Cosby shoot was, I assure you, no vacation. Can you imagine anything worse than Crawford?

Well, here it comes.

When Cosby agreed to perform in the spot, he asked to co-write it with me. I had never agreed to these kinds of things. When you're a writer, giving control to someone else could be a disaster. They don't know the marketing idea. They don't particularly care about the history of the brand, or the legal implications. And they've never written anything to fit in a 30-second format.

But this time, I put those concerns aside. Who could be a better writer for Cosby than Cosby? A world-class comedian who writes most of his own material is going to help write the spot. The commercial was about angst. And who did angst better than Cosby?

"So David," Bill says on the phone, "come out a week early and we'll work on it together."

Normally, in the advertising business, you write a script months in advance, so the client and network can approve it. Cosby insists a week is all he's got to create and film. The client agrees to this abbreviated schedule. A month later, I fly out to Las Vegas where Cosby's performing on the strip and call him:

"Meet me tonight for dinner in the nightclub before the show. We'll get started. "

I show up at the hotel's huge nightclub and find the stage-side table. I discover there are already two gorgeous young women there. No Cosby. I think I'm at the wrong table. I'm assured this is the right table and these are his friends, Hilly and Silly, from somewhere or other, clearly seeking stardom. Bill shows up presently.

He introduces me to the giggling young things. Drinks come, and I expect them to leave after their giggling sips of bubbly so we can work, but they remain for the duration. We get absolutely nothing done.

Bill gets up to prepare for his performance, apologizes for the lost evening, and says we'll definitely get it done tomorrow. He'll do some thinking about it before then. I watch Cosby on stage. He's got "Cosby" down, but I'm getting nervous.

The next night, when I show up for dinner, Bill is already at the table alone. *"Good. He's had some thoughts and we'll get to work."* Just then, two even more startlingly beautiful women join us. Don't know who they are. But more drinks, more laughs. Dinner comes. *"The girls will leave now, I hope."* But they don't. I'd ask them to leave, but I find it difficult to be rude. I say to myself, *"Hey, girls, Bill and I are supposed to be writing a commercial tonight and my life depends on it."* I say it to myself, but I don't say it to them. Another evening is lost.

"Boy, the evening got away from us. Definitely tomorrow, don't worry." says Bill.

I am in full panic now. It's Wednesday morning and the shoot is Friday. Should I start writing the script on my own? Will Cosby think that's a presumption. Will it sour him to the project? I wait nervously for dinner.

I call the agency, who tells the client — who had expected the spot last night — to expect the spot tomorrow morning. In New York, they are beside themselves, but not nearly as much as I am.

Wednesday night and there are no girls. Thank heavens. We begin to discuss the story line for the spot. Suddenly, Joe and Flo from Ko-ko-mo plop themselves down. "Jeez, David, I forgot all about them." Bill begins to discuss the commercial with all of us at the table. Flo has some brilliant ideas — or so she thinks. After all, she was an English major at University of South Podunk. Bill apologizes, but the evening is a waste.

I can't believe it. It's now Thursday. The shoot is Friday. I get a call from Bill in the morning. I'm delighted. I think to myself, *"Wonderful! He knows we've wasted several days. He's going to want to get together now, so we have all day to work."*

Instead, I hear, "David, I'm a little under the weather today, but I know you've really gotten a good sense of me over the last few days, so why don't you write the spot yourself and we'll polish it in the morning."

I've never had a panic attack, but someone once told me what it feels like and I think this is my first. My face is numb. I'm in a cold sweat. I can hear my heart pounding in my ears. I am a dead bird. Out of regard for Bill, I have purposely not made any effort to think about a script ahead of him. I have no ideas. There are about six working hours between me and the time the script needs to be sent off to the clients in New York. It's either that or the end of the world.

"OK, David," I whimper to myself, *"you're on your own."* For 15 minutes I sit there blankly. My only thoughts are of what my next job might be. Then—*"Will there be a next job? Will the advertising world learn of this and will my career be over?"*

In time, my head clears. I begin to focus. I write the spot. To my surprise, it's quite funny. I'm elated. How on earth I got something even coherent written under all this pressure amazes me. I send it to New York. I get a return call at about 9:00 p.m. It's midnight in New York. The client loves it. The spot is approved. I'm saved.

The next morning starts quite early. The crew assembles, Bill arrives, he reads the script and laughs, and we begin to shoot. Things are going brilliantly. By 11 o'clock, it's clear the spot is a major success.

At 12:15 p.m., I'm called to the phone. "David, really bad news." Bad news, at this late date, what could be bad news? "Really, really bad news. The network censors have disapproved the commercial." Censors? Disapproved? This can't be happening.

In those days, the networks employed censors to police whether advertising claims were honest and not misleading, and whether language was appropriate for TV, etc. (I remember once writing a commercial with a parody of General Patton. His famous words "War is hell" were intoned in the spot. The censors came back with "War is heck." Really. Heck? Golly, guys, America's most pugnacious general is suddenly Mr. Rogers?

Back then, the censors could be utterly impossible when clearing spots for even a run of the mill commercial. Ironically, even in those days, you could do nothing to censor, or even fact-check, political advertising. Political speech is protected by the First Amendment. Remarkable. Make a vaguely misleading claim about an underarm deodorant and it's back to the drawing board. Tell a whopper about your opponent in a political spot, and they elect you president.

Back to the disastrous situation at hand. We had gotten approval from the censors months ago for the campaign direction. Both the David Niven and Joan Crawford spots had been approved. How could this be?

Indeed, the censor on this day had decided that the language in the spot was arousing fear of flying rather than acknowledging it. (God forbid we arouse fear. Political commercials never did that!) If this were two months before the shoot, we'd have our lawyers negotiate with the censors to find some common ground. But the cameras were already rolling. This was no time for argument. I had to write another spot right this second.

At 12:30 p.m., halfway through the shoot, with a million dollars' worth of cast and crew shuffling from one foot to the other, I sat down to write another commercial.

As I look back now, I have no idea how I was able to survive the pressure or write a spot that was even coherent. If there was ever a time for my mind to go blank, this was it. But somehow it didn't. My hands were shaking, but by 3 o'clock the spot was written and approved by clients and censor. By 7 o'clock, Cosby had put in an inimitable performance. It was a memorable spot.

Years later, Cosby was incarcerated on accusations of rape. That day, I felt that a crime had been committed on me. As I write this years later, I feel the beginnings of another panic attack.

The Great Fiat Non-Meeting

I didn't always work with Amil on commercials. At one point, I partnered with another exceptional art director: Roy Grace.

Roy had created some of the most famous commercials in advertising history at DDB for Alka Seltzer ("Spicy Meatballs"), Volkswagen ("Funeral"), and American Tourister ("Gorilla"). You may not know them by name but look them up on YouTube. They are three of the greatest TV commercials of their time. You'll enjoy them.

Ally, at the time, was at the top of the industry in terms of reputation. Even Roy Grace, coming off legendary successes at DDB, wanted to work there. And I was fortunate enough to become his creative partner.

This story is about Roy and me, but it's not about creating commercials. It's a story about the sheer silliness and politics within large corporations.

One Friday afternoon, out of the blue, I received a call from Fiat Europe.

"David," I'm told by this officious official, "it is very important that you and Mr. Grace, as the representatives of Fiat in the United States, attend a meeting this Monday morning at 9:00 a.m. in Torino." (Hey, it's Friday, dude!) "Do not worry. We've arranged a flight for you both on Sunday at 6:00 p.m. from Kennedy airport. We have worked out all the details. You'll arrive at 7:00 a.m. Monday morning in Torino, a driver will meet you at the airport and take you to the Hotel Principe Piemonte, (a stunning palace of a hotel,) where he'll wait for you to refresh yourself for an hour, and then he'll drive you to the meeting. Being on time for this meeting is urgently important."

It seemed like an odd and mysterious, and certainly last-minute, request. But Fiat was odd and mysterious and last-minute. This was a time of executive kidnappings in Italy, and several times I was driven to a meeting where there was no meeting only to be driven to someplace else for the actual meeting. This was not simple paranoia. People were being held for ransom. However, since they weren't actively abducting Jewish copywriters from New York, I felt reasonably safe.

On this day, there were no kidnappings of any kind. Everything worked like clockwork. We arrived at the meeting at 9:00 a.m. precisely, and we were immediately ushered into the largest conference room I've ever seen. The single table sat about 50. The room was ornamented in the severe art deco style popular in the 1930s and '40s. I had no doubt that this had been one of Mussolini's conference rooms. The formality of the room was reflected in the still life placed in front of each chair — a tiny flag of each representative's country, (I never knew before what the flag of Yugoslavia or Belgium looked like), a small pitcher and glass of water, a yellow, lined pad, and three pencils freshly sharpened to precisely the same length. Clearly, this was a serious meeting.

As a group, each of the marketing and advertising professionals from every one of the countries where Fiat was sold entered the room and took his seat. I say "his" because there was not a woman in the room. Save for a few, almost no one spoke a common language. We sat there in silence. By 9:30 a.m., a half-hour after we had all arrived, everyone was staring at the doors, restless in his seat, then turning to the three empty chairs at the head of the table to see whether someone had arrived and we had missed it. Ten more minutes went by, no one appeared. Another 20 minutes went by. This was beyond rude.

At precisely 10 o'clock, three men entered. Neither Roy, nor I, nor my comrades at the table (judging from their blank expressions,) had any idea who these three very tardy men were.

They do not introduce themselves. They are so important; they need no introduction.

One begins to speak in Italian. We anticipate a translation. None comes. We listen some more, still no translation.

Roy, sitting next to me, squeezes my knee. I look at him. His face is bright red. He is trying to suppress his laughter. Could what appears to be happening really be happening? Could we have been flown halfway across the world to a meeting featuring unintelligible gibberish? This meeting is probably costing them a million dollars in airfare and hotels.

I bite my cheeks to keep from roaring. I look across the table and see most of the representatives from across the world also have no idea what is being said. They are squirming in their seats. They try to avert their eyes from each other for fear that mutual recognition of what's going on will put us all over the edge. My cheeks are bitten raw, but I cannot, I must not, laugh. My thigh is now bruised from Roy's squeezing.

The meeting ends at 11:00 a.m., precisely one hour after it began. The three men stand up, one nods acknowledgement to the audience, the other two just turn on their heels and they leave. There is no further explanation, no translation, nothing.

We look for someone in the room who appears to understand Italian and can tell us what just transpired. We find someone, but he tells us something in English so broken we don't understand any more than before.

We leave for the U.S. that evening without the slightest idea of what's been said.

When we arrive at the office in New York, the management supervisor on the Fiat account rushes up to us and nervously asks about the meeting. What momentous news has been imparted? What action is to be taken? Surely, we weren't all fired? We tell him we have no idea. It requires a moment for him to take this in. He appears confused, then a light goes on. He shrugs his shoulders.

"Well, that's the Italians." he says.

Over the years, I've come to understand our account guy was right:

That is the Italians. Italians revel in grandiose gestures, as if life is an opera. They use these public opportunities to put themselves in the spotlight, to demonstrate their power, and to establish some advantage over their peers. I once asked the marketing director of one of our other Italian clients, Tic Tac, about this behavior. Alberto was one of the many brilliant marketing intellectuals in Europe. A wry smile came to his lips—

"David," he said, "you must remember, Machiavelli was an Italian."

Poor People's Campaign

IN February and March 1968, Martin Luther King began to organize what would be known as the "Poor People's Campaign." I was lucky enough to be chosen to write the only advertisements for this historic venture.

The plight of the unrepresented, the poor, and the powerless was the central theme of Martin Luther King's life. It manifested itself in multiple protests and marches, and it gave birth to the idea of a Poor People's Campaign.

The concept was simple and daring: to bring thousands of poor people to Washington, so that Congress would be confronted by the reality of their poverty.

In Dr. King's own words: "They should say, 'We are here, we are poor, we don't have any money: you have made us this way... and we've come to stay until you do something about it... We are coming to ask America to be true to the huge promissory note that it signed years ago. And we are coming to engage in a dramatic non-violent action, to call attention to the gulf between promise and fulfillment.' "

King's plan was to construct a tent city on the National Mall to be known as Resurrection City. Then, he would lead a nationwide march on Washington on April 22 to pressure Congress to pass legislation addressing unemployment, housing, and the devastating effects of endemic poverty.

On April 4, a few, short weeks before the planned march, Dr. King was assassinated. All of us who were alive then recall the day; this was a historically dark moment. There was violence in major cities across America. The direction the country would take was hanging in the balance. With the death of Dr. King, it appeared that so much hope and so much promise — including the Poor People's Campaign — would disappear. In the face of this, on April 16, Rev. Ralph Abernathy held a retreat where the campaign resolved to carry on.

A "Committee of 100" from the Campaign went to Congress to plead its case and propose an economic bill of rights. Sadly, it included many of the things poor people are still fighting for: a meaningful job at a living wage, adequate income for those who are unable to find a job, access to capital for minorities to grow their own businesses, to promote their own businesses, and the opportunity for ordinary people to have a significant role in government.

In 1968, the plight of poor people in America was much lower on Congress' agenda than the issue of Vietnam. The Committee of 100 had little sway with Congress. What more could they do to gain attention? The idea of a major manifesto in the form of a full-page ad emerged. The hope was that this advertisement, which would announce the issue to the nation alongside its morning coffee, might have an effect. Well, they'd tried everything else.

While hundreds of thousands would see the ad in the New York Times and Washington Post, the purpose was not to simply sway public opinion. The principal audience for this ad was Congress.

Taking Dr. King's Bill of Rights as direction, I wrote and Ron Barrett took on the art direction. As I look back, I was not fully aware of the historical significance of this single ad. Had I truly understood how much was riding on it, frankly, I might not have been able to write a word. After much thinking and re-thinking, I completed the copy, and with the photograph and headline in place, we were ready to meet.

A date was arranged to present the ad to Rev. Abernathy at Tent City. When we arrived, the Mall was a muddy mess. (Woodstock was nothing compared to this. And there was no music.) It had been raining for days. The sea of tents and cardboard shacks was ankle-deep in mud. The sense of hopelessness was overwhelming. I remember reading the ad aloud to Rev. Abernathy while we were both standing in the quagmire. The copy, I thought, was quite moving. Ron's visual treatment of the ad was brilliant. It was a stark black and white photo of an impoverished black woman standing in the middle of a one-room shack whose walls were covered with newspaper to keep the weather out. The photo was taken by Bruce Davidson, one of America's great photojournalists, while he was on a documentary tour of the South. This was a visual of poverty unknowable to legislators and, in fact, foreign to much of America. It gave credence to the headline: "When you're poor for a day, you get hungry. When you're poor for a life, you get numb."

I felt guilty that I was writing about something that I had never experienced, but only read about, and could only imagine. The copy was moving, but quite long since it not only attempted to depict abject poverty but provide economic solutions for it. As I read the copy to Abernathy, both of us standing in the mud, I was concerned that he'd lose interest. But he stood there utterly attentive and clearly moved. At the end of my recitation of the copy, I held my breath. He hesitated to mull it over for a moment. I wondered whether he'd wish to soften some of the statements in it. Some of the demands it made on behalf of those who had nothing were large and sweeping. This was tough stuff. Instead, he offered me a sad smile, congratulated me, and told me how much it expressed Dr. King's point of view. We shook hands and I walked away with our ad intact — not a word changed — which surprised me because there was so much copy and so much riding on it.

The ad ran, and the public response was very strong and very positive. (Not everyone was supportive to those asking for "a hand up, not a hand out.") The Campaign got a lot of mail, and unreserved praise from a number of Congressmen.

In the end, however, Congress was not sufficiently moved to immediately put forward legislation. The fate of the Campaign was sealed on June 5 when one of the PPC's principal supporters, Robert Kennedy, was assassinated. Resurrection City closed two weeks later and this sad chapter in American history ended.

I gave up on trying to have an effect on Congress for some time.

Twenty-five years later, I tried again. This time, along with several other high-profile ad executives, we lobbied Congress for support in an effort to dramatically limit campaign spending. I believed then, as I believe now, the source of most political corruption in America is the obscene amount of money that fills the coffers of candidates and elected officials. I have this seen this money used to run negative commercials that attack the competition, often falsely, with no one in sight taking responsibility for the ugly and misleading messages. Political advertising has become a story from *The Wizard of Oz*. The group funding it and the candidate profiting from it all hide behind the wizard's curtain. How many favors must be promised to gain political support?

Our idea behind going to Washington was two-fold: to establish severe campaign spending limits on all elections and to create a publicly-funded presidential race that would last several weeks, not many months. We proposed that during this period, candidates would create a proscribed number of commercials. Each commercial would feature the candidate on camera articulating a specific position on an individual issue: the economy, jobs, foreign policy, etc. The two candidates' spots would run back-to-back so the voter could compare their positions. At the end of it all, the public would be voting on what the candidates actually stood for, not who uttered the best sound bite, or smeared the competition most effectively. Each spot would be like a mini-debate.

As one might expect, we were no more successful in changing campaign spending limits, and campaign format than we had been with the Poor People's Campaign.

What was appalling was that so many in Congress hid behind the First Amendment, self-righteously feigning outrage: "To limit spending is to limit speech." Even so, we were able to rally a handful of legislators to our side and perhaps our efforts had a small effect on some of them.

When this country was founded, patriots gave up their careers as farmers, silversmiths, and newspapermen in order to serve their country. It was understood to be for a limited time; until they could return to their families and resume their livelihoods. Today, those in Congress view political office as a lifetime career. They care more about their own re-election and extending their careers in office than they do about the interests of their constituents. They are their own most important constituents. And there is no doubt, this situation is much worse today than when I attempted to change things. This may be the greatest country on earth, but in many ways, it is not nearly as great as we pretend. We are a work in progress, and there are times it seems like we're progressing backwards.

A Multi-National
Commercial Fiasco

YOU see a lot of car commercials on TV. They look easy, but they can be very complicated. If you're working with Italians, they can make you tear your hair out.

I worked on the Fiat account for close to a decade in both Europe and America. I created a number of commercials for Fiat that were shot on the Continent. Shooting there was both wonderful and terrible. Wonderful because the food and the cities and country-side were amazing. Terrible because — well, you'll see.

For this particular commercial, when I say, "shot on the Continent," I mean shot *all over* the Continent: Italy, Spain, France, Switzerland, Germany, Scandinavia. The strategy of the spot was to introduce this great Italian car company to America by promoting its overwhelming popularity across just about every country in Europe. The spot was created to visually dramatize the fact that in this large diverse group of countries, where there is a wide disparity of driving conditions, different cultural demands, different topography, and dramatically diverse requirements for a car, Fiat was the best-selling car in all of Europe. Not just now, but for the last 13 straight years. An amazing fact. (Amazing facts are good.)

After we came up with the idea for the commercial, we bid it out to a well-known Italian director with whom the agency had enjoyed great success. All went well in the trans-Atlantic discussions on the phone, and we awarded the job to his company.

When we arrived in Rome for a pre-production meeting a week before we were to begin shooting, things changed. We were informed that the director we had spoken to on the phone for all these weeks was suddenly not available for the shoot. Huh?

How could this be? Sadly, he was on another assignment that had taken too long, and they'd offered us another director in his place.

This is simply not something a production company ever does. Never. The director is the reason you go to the production company in the first place. They waited to inform us until we got to Rome, I imagine, so we'd be totally committed to the shoot date and subsequent air date and we couldn't back out. Utterly outrageous, but here we were in Rome and up against it.

We asked to see the replacement director's reel. It was OK. *Just* OK. Not even close to the excellence of the director we thought we had hired. We told them the replacement director was unacceptable. (Or more precisely, "Are you fuckin' kidding?") They were insulted. That was fine because we were infuriated. After some testy discussion, they countered with "What if we can get you a great director of photography?" On this kind of commercial where we were filming cars in various countries, in all sorts of driving situations — horrendous traffic jams, driving down narrow alleys built for donkey carts not cars, traversing mountain switchbacks, bumping through unpaved terrain — it was evident that the right Director of Photography (commonly known as "camera man") would be even more important than the right director. There were no actors to direct, just cars. There were no stages, just locations to shoot.

We said, "OK, let's see who you can get."

Remarkably, they came back with one of the most highly regarded cinematographers in the world, Vittorio Storaro. Storaro was, and is, legend. He was Bertolucci's cameraman on most of his films including *Last Tango in Paris*. He won the Academy Award for Cinematography for *Apocalypse Now, Reds*, and *The Last Emperor*. Storaro is the cinematographer of your dreams. The question was not whether we'd use him, the question was how on earth did they get him?

We delightedly agreed to move forward with the stand-in, second-rate director, and star camera man. But there were more surprises.

The next day, at the pre-production meeting, we learned that our new stand-in, second-rate director doesn't fly. A director who doesn't fly? Next, they'll provide a translator who only speaks Bulgarian. This was a commercial that was supposed to be filmed all over Europe.

"How were we to get from Spain, to France, to Germany, to Switzerland, to Italy?"

"It is a car commercial, David. We drive."

"Drive? Thousands of miles across Europe? And when will we be seeing the scouting pictures of all the locations we're driving to?"

"Oh, we are not 'sounting.' We get up very early, every day, and drive until we find the perfect location. Then, we shoot." ("Sounting" is the way the Italians pronounced it. From this team's behavior, it was clear they had little experience with doing it.)

I couldn't imagine anything more reckless. Without any advance planning, they actually intended to mobilize an entourage of twenty "hero" Fiats, plus multiple crew cars and equipment trucks, and drive thousands of miles back and forth across Europe until they found the perfect locations. How crazy is this?

"This is going to cost a fortune," we said, "and besides that, it could take forever."

"We understand your concern, David. We guarantee the cost of the shoot. However long it takes, it takes."

We were worried, and we made it utterly clear that there'd not be another penny given when they went over budget—which we were convinced they would—and we'd make no compromises in the quality of what we shot for the sake of expediency. With these assurances, we very reluctantly agreed to move forward, and two days later we were on our way.

The entourage drove from Rome to Genoa, a large port city on the west coast of Italy and boarded a cargo ship there. We filled the hold with our fleet of vehicles, lights, rigging, and camera equipment, and set sail overnight across the Mediterranean to Barcelona, where the shoot was to begin. And when I say fleet of vehicles, I mean *fleet*. Beyond the camera cars and equipment trucks, there were the cars for all the production personnel, plus the 20 Fiats that would be the stars of the shoot. If these had been armed vehicles, we would be ready to start a war.

When we arrived in Barcelona, we received our next surprise. How many surprises can you take? The production company had not thought ahead to get shooting permits for what was clearly a major venture, and as a result, as we attempted to exit the ship, the government impounded our trucks and equipment. How you organize a battalion of vehicles to arrive in an autocracy like Francoist Spain without permits is inconceivable. The government, now in the last years of the Franco regime, was convinced that this commercial was really some anti-government propaganda film. And given the politics in Spain at the time, who could blame them?

We appealed to Fiat Corporate in Italy to do something on our behalf. As one of Europe's largest and most powerful companies, we figured approval was simply a matter of time. It proved true, but it took plenty of time. Franco, for good reason, was quite paranoid about bad press.

Every morning, for six days, we came down for breakfast from our rooms in one of Barcelona's grand hotels and learned that authorization was not coming that day.

"How sad. Let's go back to sleep."

Then, we'd go for an outrageously expensive lunch and see the sights. You have no idea how many grand hotels and residences Antoni Gaudi designed in Barcelona.

They have been building the great cathedral of Barcelona, Gaudi's Sagrada Familia since 1866 and they're still not done. We had a feeling that this shoot might go the same way.

You would be amazed at how many ways the chefs of Barcelona can prepare shellfish. This was also the first time I'd experienced tapas. It was a life-changing experience.

You also can't fathom how much money was wasted on luxury and excess on commercial shoots back then (I say was, because these days, while excess still exists, it is far less excessive.)

After those six days of dining and sightseeing, the Spanish government concluded we were not attempting a coup, and our entourage was released from impound.

At last, we headed into the interior of Spain seeking the look of a country before superhighways, in fact, before roads. We sure found them. The interior of Spain looked much like one imagines the 18th century. Sometimes, there were more burros on the roads than cars. Every day, we began driving before sunrise looking for the perfect mountain to climb, the perfect stream to wade through, the perfect sheep to just miss hitting. Scouting? Who needs scouting?

Now, you should understand that if you want images to look beautiful on film, you shoot at beginning or end of day. In the film business, the light at those times is called "golden light." Noonday sun burns out everything and makes images look harsh and ugly. So, when do you suppose we came upon the perfect location to shoot every day? You guessed it: just about noon. Time to break for lunch.

"Can't shoot now, let's eat."

We soon realized the one thing on the shoot that the Italian crew scouted best was the place to eat lunch. Every day, sometime early in the morning, they would send out a crew to search the neighboring 30 miles for the best restaurant. No, the Italians couldn't waste their time scouting for places to shoot, but they sure could scout for the best places to eat. Sometimes these places were a half-hour away, an hour there and back. But what's time in the pursuit of a good meal?

Thus, every day we'd drive a long distance, have a leisurely and spectacular lunch, and get back by 3:30 p.m. If this were June or July, when the sun sets quite late in the evening in Europe, 4 o'clock wouldn't be too bad. But this was November, when the sun was down by 5:00 p.m. So, finally back at the location the crew would scramble out of the trucks, set up cameras, and rush to get a shot before we lost light. All this travel, all this cost for one shot a day or two—if we were lucky. If there was some problem with the weather, or the camera, or the star vehicle, no shots a day. At this rate, we would be shooting until next April. This was a gorgeous shot, no doubt. But one shot? With no back up?

I remember, late in the shoot, we had a lunch on a very cold and rainy day in Bresse, France. We had been up to our knees in mud trudging about looking for the perfect location. (This was one of our "car slogging through mud" shots.) We were frozen and hungry with pants wet up to our knees. At noon precisely, shortly after we came upon the perfect spot, we left the location, got into our cars, and were driven to this little inn about a half hour away. I'm not sure whether it was because we were starving from a morning out in the cold, but they served us — without question — the best roast chicken in the history of the world. Whatever my mother called "chicken," this was a different species. I later learned that "poulet de Bresse" is regarded as the best chicken in Europe — perhaps the world. Maybe the reason we were shooting there was not for the beauty of the landscape, but for the beauty of the truffle-stuffed bird that followed the monster antipasto and Tortellini in Brodo. Which were nothing to sneeze at either.

After a steady diet of these lengthy lunches, I began complaining vehemently. "As lovely as this is, we can't keep doing this," I said, with great passion. "We can't spend three hours at lunch and a half hour shooting. We have to eat at the location. We need to bring sandwiches along."

The crew looked at me as if I was from Mars. Sandwich? Sandwich?? Where were my priorities? Was I a barbarian? There were no takers to the sandwich idea. They got more worked up about the mere thought of this than anything on the shoot. The best I could get from them was that they'd *try* to look for restaurants closer to the location.

I came to realize that the Italian mentality is quite different from ours. (I learned this many times in the course of the shoot.) For them, work is something you do to eat well. If you can't eat well, why work?

I also learned that Italians never say no.

"Will you do this tomorrow?"

"Sure, sure."

When it didn't happen, "Oh. It was a problem."

"Can you do it tomorrow?"

"Sure, sure."

They never actually said "no" to the sandwich idea, they just never acted on it. I was never able to end the noon-time lunch treks. The driving distances were sometimes shorter, but the lunches were never short. We solved some of the problems, on occasion, by scouting the next day's locations in advance on the way to lunch so we could get some shots in the next day's morning light, but lunchtime was their time. With travel, lunch time was never less than two and a half to three hours.

Ultimately, when we finally got to Rome, the producer, to whom I had been constantly complaining, greeted me in great excitement.

"Today, David," she said triumphantly, " we give you what you have been asking for: a box lunch."

Really? Now they get it?

At noon precisely, a large truck pulled up at the location. This was not a small, panel truck; this was something the size of an Allied moving van. From out of the truck came the mother of all box lunches, individually packed for 40: a box of prosciutto and melon, a box of spaghetti amatriciana (piping hot), a box of saltimbocca or veal scallopini (your choice), a box of green salad with little cups of dressing, a box of panna cotta with a box of chocolate sauce, individual bottles of the excellent local wine and sparkling water, and a tiny bottle of Fernet Branca. With all those boxes of food you needed a digestive.

Needless to say, by the time the tables and chairs were unloaded from the truck and set up, the hundreds of little boxes were carefully distributed, the huge meal consumed, and the empty boxes and tables and chairs reloaded on the truck, the lunch lasted longer than if we'd gone to another country for it.

Dinner was an even more tumultuous spectacle. At least it was dark and there were no shots to stress over. All 40 of us would descend on a small country restaurant en masse. We'd often take over the entire place. Dinner would go on until late in the night.

On many nights, sometime during dinner, some kind of craziness would ensue. (Like everything else in this book, this is absolutely true.) One of our group would take a small piece of bread and roll it into a tiny ball and throw this little bread version of a spitball at someone else at the table. (You can't make these things up.) A bread ball was fired back. Suddenly it was an all-out bread ball war. Even guests at the neighboring tables weren't safe. I recall one night in the mountains of Switzerland, the battle of the bread balls moved outside and escalated into an epic snowball fight. It began with the drivers — most of them retired policemen — and grew until everyone from the restaurant was pummeling each other outside in the snow. It went on for what seemed like hours. I realized that these weren't just policemen, they were oversized 10-year-olds. Any notion of decorum went out the window. We could be at the fanciest restaurant for miles around and mayhem would be assured.

***

Managing only one shot, at best, two shots a day, any notion of a timetable was a wildly optimistic dream. The shoot, which began in mid-November and was scheduled to last two weeks, was now passing six weeks.

On Christmas morning, I awoke early to see what everyone was up to on this holiday. I discovered that the crew was nowhere to be found. They had simply left for Christmas to be with their families back home. No one informed the Americans. They just *left*.

I mention this because more than any other group of people I've ever met, the Italians were filled with an impossible joie de vivre. (I bet there's an Italian word for that kind of "joie." I bet they have 10 words for it, like Eskimos have 50 for snow.) Sadly, it didn't translate into a *"joie de responsabilité"*

One amazing thing did happen on that Christmas morning. With no work in sight, the few Americans in our group decided to go to St. Peter's Basilica. We expected the usual Christmas ritual; to stand with thousands of Italians in Vatican Square to receive the Pope's blessing from his balcony above. Instead, when we arrived, people were not standing in the square. The doors of St. Peter's were open. and people were streaming in. Once inside, we saw purple ropes being put along the aisles, and suddenly hundreds of nuns appeared and pressed against them. Next, I saw something I never expected to ever see. At the end of a long procession of clerical folk, Pope Paul VI was carried into the church on a huge golden throne to preside over his first public Christmas mass in a language other than Latin. There was so much pomp on that day, had you said to me, "David, would you like to give up all that Jewish stuff and sign up to be Catholic?" I would have signed on the dotted line without hesitation. For the first time, I understood why cathedrals were built with so much grandeur. With the soaring organ music, the candles, and the huge choir and the ceremonies conducted with such sheer power and beauty; this was seduction on a scale I had never seen. I expect I'll not see anything like that again.

Several days later, the crew returned as if nothing had happened, and the insanity recommenced. The next day, the director found "the perfect house" for one of the Fiats to drive past. The owner of the house, for whatever reason didn't want us anywhere near his property. Did this house look like it was worth fighting over as a location? Not to me.

"But this is the place we've been looking for," pleaded the director. "Get off my land," bellowed the homeowner. This was clearly no ordinary homeowner. How would they resolve this?

Shortly, a small army of the owner's relatives appeared at the windows brandishing rifles. Could a war be waged over a location? Well, the Italians did create the word "machismo." The standoff continued for about an hour until the local mafia boss finally arrived. (Yes, in Italy, every small town had a mafia boss, or so it seemed. That's how government ran.) After a few minutes of frantic gesturing on both sides, the altercation was resolved, money passed hands, and the shoot went on without anybody being literally shot.

After another several weeks, our story finally came to an end. Thanks to Vittorio Storaro, (not our fear-of-flying director), the footage we brought back to America was stunning. To my surprise, the production company lived up to its promise. They did not hit us up for another penny. No "sure, sure." They didn't even attempt it. After a mad rush to edit all the footage, (and there was a ton of it) the commercial went on air on time and won major advertising awards both in Europe and America. If they gave an award for lunch, there's no question we would have several more prizes at the Cannes Film Festival.

What I took away from the shoot was a lesson from the Italians that I've never forgotten and have tried to live by ever since:

In the end, life is more important than work.

Remy Julienne

SHOOTING commercials doesn't always work out as you expect. There can be some ugly and expensive surprises. Sometimes the real creativity is how you deal with disasters.

About halfway in my tenure at Ally, Amil and I created a sequel to a Fiat spot made years earlier. The original spot featured a world-famous stunt driver, Remy Julienne, in a classic car chase like the one filmed in *The French Connection*. In the first Fiat spot, the car lurches down the steps of a church and hurtles onto a ferry as it exits the dock. These were true daredevil stunts. It was one of the great commercial film tours de force of its time. The spot won all sorts of awards and improved Fiat's reputation in the United States dramatically.

The sequel that we envisioned would take these stunts much, much further. Remy would attempt things that the first spot never dreamed of: a car leaping from one impossibly tall mountain, hundreds of feet through the air, to land gracefully atop another; plummeting down a steep waterfall and falling fifty feet into a river and then righting itself as it broke the water and floating gracefully down the fast-moving rapids; hurtling like a ski jumper off a steep slope, landing squarely on its wheels 200 feet further down the hill; and driving through an open boxcar door on a train traveling at 50 miles an hour, into one side of the train and then exiting out the other. Crazy, dangerous things.

As Remy conceptualized these stunts, they seemed more and more dangerous. He worked for days doing all sorts of mathematical calculations. Remy assured us he would not try a stunt unless the physics of it made it an utter certainty. It would look impossibly daring, but nevertheless, it would be foolproof. Based on these assurances, we moved forward with some trepidation. Here's what happened.

First stunt: Remy gets the car to a speed of 70 miles per hour, he becomes airborne from mountain one, and the car flies gracefully through the air. (We shoot it in super-slow motion like an automotive ballet.) The car lands squarely in the side of mountain two. Not on top of it—right into it. *Splat!* The entire front of the car is crushed. We rush to the car thinking Remy must be dead. We pry open the driver's door and there he is smiling sheepishly. Somehow, and I still don't know how, Remy walks away with only his forehead and ego bruised. He missed the top of the mountain by more than five feet. The miscalculation was so great, we should have cancelled the rest of the stunts. Remy was clearly not so good at math. But he assures us the next ones will go perfectly. It's his life. We proceed to the next stunt.

Second stunt: Remy drives his Fiat into the river, floats down about 50 feet to the rapids and the car is carried over the falls. It perches for a moment horizontally, one end hanging 30 feet above the drop, then lurches forward and heads straight down. The car lands smack on its nose. Once again, the whole front end of the car is crushed. After what seems an eternity, the car bobs to back the surface and so does Remy. Two for two.

Third stunt: The car speeds down the ski slope doing a vehicular slalom Suddenly, instead of zigging or zagging, it rolls over onto its side and tumbles, side over side, 100 feet down the slope. If it weren't so frightening, this would begin to be amusing.

Five stunts are attempted. Five disasters. At one point, to our shock, Remy sends his twenty-something year old son to attempt a stunt. Has he begun to doubt himself? Enough to put his son at risk of death?

Things never got better, but Remy and his son lived. That's the good part. But the question was: What do we do with all this beautiful footage of these very ugly accidents? Do we scrap the shoot as a foolhardy and expensive mistake? Does the agency take a huge financial hit in eating the cost of a failed half million dollar production? Is there a way to salvage this horror show?

In the midst of screening the frightening footage, we have an idea! A much more creative thought than doing the stunts in the first place. We edit each accident as a single commercial in all its cover-your-eyes awfulness. The disasters are riveting. Then Remy, voice over, tells us that—for his own survival—he will only attempt these stunts in a Fiat. *Poof!* From failed daredevil spots, we turn them into truly powerful safety spots.

In the script, where the car does the nose-dive over the falls and into the river, we hear Remy say: "People ask me whether I do these stunts with Fiats for money. Tell me, would you do this for money?"

You got a lemon, make lemonade.

The Ally Postmortem

YEARS after I left to start my own agency, Ally still had great personal meaning for me for me.

At their 25th anniversary party, Amil asked me to say a few words. At this point, I had been gone from the agency for over 10 years, but I had a continuing close relationship with Amil and my old colleagues there. It was a sad event because after its brilliant run, after all its marketing and creative successes, the agency had lost a number of clients in quick succession and was forced to close its doors. It had been an incredible 25 years.

Much of the work was industry-changing. I, and many of my compatriots, had left to start successful agencies of our own — Ed McCabe, Ralph Ammirati and Marty Puris, Roy Grace, Dick Raboy, Tom Messner, Barry Vitere, and Ron Berger. (If you were in the business, you'd know these names well.) Given the trail of landmark work and success for its clients, and the great agencies it had spawned, how had the end for Ally come so soon? Why were so many agencies with great, creative pedigrees dying and those with a legacy of utter mediocrity continuing to thrive?

I continue to believe the remarks I made at that party so long ago are true:

"The agencies that creatively burned the most brightly ultimately were consumed in their own flames. The creative support they demanded of their clients was given for a period of time and taken back. The agencies were more interested in what they considered great work than great relationships built upon mediocre work. It was just too hard for some clients to live on that edge interminably. Given what these agencies demanded of their clients, it was inevitable that most of the agency stars of that time have been extinguished—Carl Ally, and Wells, Rich, Green, Scali, McCabe and Sloves, Ammirati and Puris—all would be gone. I say this with great sadness. These were the bright shining lights of their time. Who would show the way now?"

I remember having lunch with Jay Chiat. He owned and ran a great agency in L.A. that emulated Carl's advertising approach. Chiat/Day did exceptional work for clients like Apple and Nike. Like Ally, the work was very demanding of client's willingness to take, and as a result, Chiat's agency was a revolving door. But unlike Ally, they fired staff as quickly as they lost business. Firing staff was what kept them afloat.

I asked Jay: "How do you manage? How do you attract staff when you've become notorious for being unstable?"

He said, "The creatives come for the quality of the work we do. They do great until we are forced to let them go. The clients? We just kind of rent them. You know, clients are never really yours. You have them for a while and the question is whether during that time you get the best of them or they get the best of you. You're going to lose them in time anyway. Will we do great work for them during that time, work we can use to attract other clients? Or will they fire us, and we end up with nothing to show for it?"

Using this boom-or-bust philosophy, Jay built a successful agency with legacy of great work. But his agency was never nearly as successful as the mediocre agencies with a legacy of forgettable work.

The agencies that made life comfortable for clients, that demanded little of them, were the places clients preferred to live. Even if the clients were to garner less fame, and their companies achieved a lesser degree of growth, for them the ease of day-to-day living with the agency was worth it.

Before I leave Carl and his extraordinary agency, I have to relate a story Carl told me about his good friend, Howard Gossage. Everybody in the business knows Bill Bernbach, but few know the name Howard Gossage. They should. Howard was a truly great writer, teacher, and small agency owner in, what was then, the backwater of advertising, San Francisco. Like Bernbach and Ally in the East, he spawned a generation of creative acolytes on the West Coast. He also was one of the first real advertising activists, which was probably what first attracted Carl to him.

Howard was, in my mind, one of the unsung geniuses in the history of the business. He wrote what may be the most understated summary of what print advertising is at its essence: "Nobody reads ads. People read what interests them. And sometimes it's an ad."

Anyway, when Howard died, Carl received a call from his widow, Dagmar. She asked him if he would fly over San Francisco Bay and shower Howard's ashes over the iconic bay of the city he loved.

So, Carl flew out to the coast and took up a small plane with Dagmar aboard. As he opened the door of the plane and threw out the ashes over the Pacific, a gust of wind lofted the ashes back into the plane and into Dagmar's lap. Without hesitation, Dagmar uttered, "Isn't that just like Howard. Still trying to get in my pants.

To all of us who knew him, Carl still gets in our pants.

On a personal note, I should say that Carl Ally, Inc. made my career. Without this exceptional agency, who knows where I might have ended up. Most likely I'd be at one of the legions of mediocre agencies similar to the ones I had come from, slogging through a career of utterly forgettable commercials. and living a cushy life in the suburbs. For me, this was not nearly enough. Like so many aspiring creative people at the time, I aspired to advertising's version of greatness. My luck, or you could say my perseverance, or you could say my willingness to go financially backwards to pursue a dream, landed me at an agency where I was not simply prodded to create good work, but where the work was stuffed down the client's throats, and as a result, actually saw the light of day.

In another speech, this time made as President of the One Show, I think I said it better: "You are only as good as the agency you work for. You can never transcend it. As a creative person, you may create the babies, but it takes an agency to have the courage to bring them into the world. I'm one of the lucky ones. I worked at a truly great agency; an agency with boundless courage. There are many exceptional creative people sitting in this audience working for lesser agencies whose best work never sees the light of day. At Ally, I had people fighting for my work every day. And that's why I'm fortunate enough to be standing here."

The Beginning of
My Own Agency

The Early Days of
Altschiller Reitzfeld

AFTER 13 years at Ally, I'd had enough.

Carl Ally was still very much in charge of the agency, but he was in the midst of a major mid-life crisis. He was battling his third wife in a very ugly divorce and to escape the daily marital struggle, he went to Europe for months at a time to tend to the European business for our clients, Pan Am and Fiat. In the end, Carl was spending more time in Europe than in New York. During Carl's absence, with my help, Amil was managing the agency, business was stable, clients were happy, and the work was good.

When Carl wandered back in the door, he showed little regard for the success that had been achieved while he was meandering around Europe. After all, in his mind, if he weren't leading the charge, how good could it be? To say the least, Carl, at this moment, was destabilizing to the agency and humiliating to us. We were not children. We didn't need poppa to come home and set things right. He was now actively setting things wrong.

At this point in my career, I had received a great deal of industry recognition. I had risen to the top of Ally and was Amil's creative partner. I couldn't go any higher in the agency. I had been named one of the top 10 copywriters in America for over a decade. I was President of the Copy Club and helped merge it with the Art Director's Club to create the most highly regarded creative organization in the industry, The One Club. I had won more awards at the various awards shows than almost anyone in the industry to date. In short, I had accomplished more than I had ever dreamed of and I was really full of myself.

Because of all the accolades, being treated like a child by Carl did not go down easily. (As I look back on it, I was just 35 years old—practically a child.) And I was determined to do something about it. Amil and I began to muse about leaving the agency together to start our own, or instead, somehow ridding the place of Carl.

At this same moment, from out of the blue, I was approached by a fellow copywriter who I really respected, Dick Jackson. Dick was one of the industry's exceptional print writers. He was now working at one of Ally's principal rivals, Wells Rich Greene, Inc. (WRG).

Dick told me that the head of new business at WRG, a man by the name of Andy Morgan, who had brought in hundreds of millions of dollars' worth of business there, was unhappy with Mary Wells and wanted to go in business with Dick.

Would I like to join them? This came as a complete surprise to me. The idea was intriguing, but I already had what might be the best creative job in the business—albeit with some frustration due to Carl.

But because of my frustration, the idea of leaving and starting my own agency with Jackson was intriguing and soon began to take on a life of its own. This was a very risky notion, but I was unhappy enough to consider it. The fact that Dick and I were both writers, and therefore redundant, didn't faze us. We focused on needing an art director at our level as a partner. We sought out a mutual friend, Barney Melsky. Barney was producer for Howard Zieff, the hottest director in the industry. If there was a great commercial created in the 1960s or `70s, there's a good chance Howard directed it. Barney knew and worked with the brightest people in agency business. We asked him to find us a brilliant art director as a potential partner. He did. Robert (Bob) Reitzfeld was his name. He was a great talent who had worked at all the right places and had an eye-opening portfolio. We knew his work well.

In the next weeks, Dick and I spent many lunches and dinners with Bob and determined that he was a good fit with us.

So here we were, three creatives: two copywriters and an art director. One more copywriter than an agency needed to start with but we had a more pressing question: was Andy Morgan, our potential new business man, real? Could he deliver business to a fledgling agency?

I was far too loyal to Ally to try to take business from them. Dick and Bob had no business they were close to. This entire venture relied on Andy Morgan to bring us clients. We had seen far too many "new businessmen" who were charlatans. They told a good story, but their prospects rarely materialized.

We had amassed a truly formidable body of work to wow prospective clients. The key was for Andy to get us in front of them.

"Andy, we don't mean to be skeptical, but we've heard this kind of story from new business people many times before. To make you part of this, we need you to produce some actual folks who are willing to meet with us and give us business"

We thought this might be the kind of assignment that he couldn't manage; arrange a business meeting with people who aren't yet in business? To Andy's credit, and our great surprise, he did it. He arranged meetings with clients from Avis, Revlon, Pepsi, and Polaroid. Andy was beginning to look like the real thing. These were major, big-budget clients. Suddenly, the agency idea was beginning to appear promising.

We were not even an agency yet, all of us were still working at our full-time jobs and meeting at Andy's apartment after work.

Since we had no office, Andy arranged meetings with these client bigwigs at his home. As I reflect on it, this was a major mistake. While we were a start-up, but not even really a start-up yet, it was foolish to look like we weren't real. We should have rented a meeting room at a hotel, borrowed offices at somebody else's agency, something more business-like. And, as you shall learn, we paid a price for the casualness of it all.

One of the first meetings Andy set up was with the marketing director of Avis. We were ecstatic. Not only was Avis big, but Avis also had enormous visibility in the advertising community. They had run a ground-breaking campaign created by Doyle Dane Bernbach: "We're number 2. We try harder." Everybody watched their ads. Why Avis might consider leaving DDB to join a fledgling agency, it never occurred to us to ask. Why didn't we?

Finally, the day to present to the Avis guy arrived. We had put together a very impressive presentation of our very impressive collective creative work.

The presentation at Andy's apartment was going very well. Then, the impossible happened.

Right in the middle of Jackson's part of the presentation, a giant cockroach emerged from behind the couch where the Avis guy was sitting and began to crawl—oh-so-slowly—across the wall behind his head. (Cockroaches are a staple of New York apartment living. Infestation is not limited to poverty-stricken slums. They're just as much at home on Park Avenue.) But this was not just a big cockroach, this was the mother of big cockroaches; a cross between a palmetto bug and a B-29. The Avis guy couldn't see it, but the four of us sitting across from him presenting sure could. How could you not? This was Roachzilla. I don't know how Jackson, who was talking at that point, didn't swallow his tongue. The rest of us were no longer listening to him because we were transfixed. The big fella finally passed behind the Avis guy's head and went down behind the couch. Whew. In unison, we breathed a silent sigh of relief. A second later, up he pops from behind the couch and makes a pass along the wall in the opposite direction. Time never passed so slowly. I was sure he'd leave the wall for a trip along the Avis fellow's left arm which was draped along the back of the couch. But he didn't. He disappeared from whence he came. I do not remember anything else from the Avis meeting.

A day later, we were informed by Andy that we did not get the Avis business (for non-roach related issues.) We should have badgered Andy about why we didn't land them, or at least a piece of their business. Was the Avis account really up for grabs? Was it simply that he agreed to make an appearance for his friend Andy but had nothing real to offer? We never pursued it. Since the entire future of this imagined agency depended on those answers, heaven knows, we should have.

At this point, my other avenue towards a departure, Amil Gargano, was having second thoughts about leaving the agency himself. To this day, I'm not sure why he decided to stay at Ally. Maybe I was more serious about truly leaving than he was. Maybe he was just grousing. Maybe he was less of a risk-taker than I. He was an original partner, so perhaps he had more loyalty to Carl. Or maybe Carl simply made promises to him I knew nothing about. (Shortly after I left, they changed the name of the agency to Ally and Gargano.) Given events soon to come, I should have stayed as well. But emotionally, I was already out the door.

I continued meeting with the guys to determine whether the Jackson idea for an agency would ever be real. Andy Morgan had now officially left WRG, so he was committed. But the other three of us were not. Why would we be? Andy had delivered no business as of yet. The agency was still nothing more than a nice idea and quite far from reality.

You should understand, the agency couldn't open its doors and simply wait for clients to come. Agencies don't do that. It's too financially risky. No client wants to be the first. Let someone else test the waters. And none of the would-be partners had stashed away enough money to fund the agency for the many months it might take to lure them. We needed to open our doors with at least one.

The plan seemed OK. There were no iron-clad commitments on any of our parts to open immediately. Everyone, except Andy, was still working, and he had a lucrative separation agreement from his former employer. We had plenty of time for Andy to bring in the right prospects and for us to make them clients before we opened our doors.

Then, something terrible happened; an event that would change the entire future of the agency and all of our lives.

Dick Jackson's plan to leave WRG and start his own business with Andy was discovered and Wells Rich Greene promptly fired him.

Just days later, Reitzfeld had an argument with the owner of the agency where he was working, and he quit. Dick and Bob both had wives and kids.

If opening the agency was to happen, it had to be immediately, or the guys had to get new jobs quick. It was now a race to bring in clients that would give the agency some kind of financial viability and establish some kind of income stream for Dick and Bob.

Andy continued to bring potential clients to meetings; clients with big jobs at big companies. What we didn't realize — and this was a major, dramatic, career-changing error on our part — is that these people were not seriously looking for new agencies. They were Andy's buddies and were doing him a favor by coming to see us. In retrospect, even if they were really impressed, most of them had nothing to give us. The bulk of their business was already spoken for at giant agencies. What they might give us were the crumbs the big guys weren't interested in. Why didn't we see this? What were we thinking? Was this a fraud on Andy's part? Was it witless, wishful thinking? Blind optimism?

So now, Reitzfeld, Morgan, and Jackson were all out of jobs. They had an ad agency with no accounts. I still had a great job, and I didn't want to jump aboard what was clearly a sinking ship. And I certainly couldn't add to their financial burden by asking for a salary, too. There was no money to go around.

So, I said to them, "If the agency gets some business and stays afloat, I'll be a silent partner. I'll stay at Ally and work with you at lunch and evenings for no pay until there's enough money for me."

Frankly, my expectation was that by the time I came aboard, the ship would either be well on its way or at the bottom of the advertising ocean.

The situation was urgent and the guys were about to take a terrible step — one that set us back years.

The agency had been conceived with expectations of Andy landing sizable clients and our growing the business by doing great work for them. Suddenly, the guys were no longer looking for major clients with decent-sized budgets for which they could do great work. This was not going to be like Carl Ally who started with Volvo, or Backer & Spielvogel who started with Miller Light, or Scali, McCabe who started with Xerox. Or Ammirati Puris who thought they were starting with Chrysler. Ours was an agency whose partners immediately had their backs to the wall, who needed any income from any source so they could eat and pay alimony.

Without question, it would have been smarter for the agency to close its doors before it ever opened. At this point, Reitzfeld and Jackson could have gone out and gotten well-paid, good jobs. They were pretty famous and eminently hirable as creative directors with big salaries. But Dick and Bob were determined to persevere. I waited in the wings to see what would transpire.

So, Andy changed his plan of attack. He went to the friends who, weeks earlier, he'd asked for major work. Now, he asked for droppings. Not accounts, but meager assignments. How much behind the scenes begging he did, we'll never know. It took several years for the agency to get to the level of client for which we'd gone into business. The life preserver allowed the boys to keep their heads financially above water, nothing more.

The agency began with newspaper ads for the department store, A&S and co-op ads from Revlon, both long time buddies of Andy's. Bless those clients, it's all they had to give. But there was a downside to this gift. The advertising tidbits required as much work and time as if they were major-sized accounts. As a result, there was now far too little time for them to pursue the clients worth having.

During this period, Ally was having its share of troubles, as well. I was happy to help Amil through them. I was working to save the agency where I was, and working nights with Morgan, Reitzfeld, and Jackson with their ill-paying handouts.

This went on for about a year. The boys struggled along, living hand-to-mouth, with me paying nightly visits. One night, totally out of the blue, Jackson said to me, "David, we really need you. You've got to join us." My response should have been, "Are you nuts?"

As I reflect on it, Dick had no right to ask. The agency could not afford to pay them, much less me. After a year, they hadn't gotten very far in attracting new business. Clearly, they had decided my addition would make a difference. I never thought this day would come.

A year earlier I had said, "When the agency is ready for me, I'll come." But the agency was nowhere near ready for me. Not by a long shot. It had little income and few immediate prospects. If I were using my brain, I would have suggested they close their doors.

I should have told Dick he had no right to ask me to board a sinking ship, but I felt I had made a promise to them. Did I promise to give up my career for them? They shouldn't have asked, but they did. And even though I knew it wasn't the right thing, I couldn't say no. I could not disappoint them.

As I reflect back on that moment, this was the worst career decision I made.

I left the safety of Ally, a job that offered great creative opportunities every day, for a fledgling agency in deep financial trouble with questionable clients.

The next five years were a relentless struggle to turn this mistake into a real agency with world-class clients like those I'd left at Ally.

Over time, the group became frustrated with Morgan and he with us. He was never the kind of marketing-oriented partner we needed. Once he brought a client into the room, he had nothing to say other than, "Meet the guys."

A short period of time after I arrived, he left. We replaced him with a bona fide marketing partner.

Accounts came, then better and better ones. Little step by little step, new business win after new business win, we grew. This was a slog, not a sprint.

But finally, we turned into the agency we hoped to be from the start. Over the next few years, we became a highly regarded mid-sized agency with larger and larger accounts.

Early on, we grew the Boar's Head provisions from a little mom and pop business in Brooklyn to the most well-known, most respected brand in the deli business.

And to wash it down, we marketed Dr. Browns sodas.

We launched Esquire Magazine. (Our slogan, "Man at his Best," has been on their masthead and is their mantra to this day.)

We helped turn Liz Claiborne from a women's clothing company into a mammoth clothing icon, and then into a fragrance icon.

We morphed Pioneer from a player in the audio business into the leader in the emerging video business.

We took Tic Tac from out-of-business in America to the leading breath mint in the country.

As our reputation grew in Italy, we signed Rocher and Mon Chéri chocolates, and then Campari.

For Post/General Foods, we created several of the biggest new product successes in the history of the cereal industry.

We created Angel Soft Bath Tissue for Georgia Pacific and turned it into a major national brand.

We created some breakthrough work for Southern Comfort.

For Perrier, we launched Poland Spring into the sparkling water business and helped people learn to pay for water.

We failed to save Polaroid.

We advertised the wonders of flying SAS, Japan Air, TAP, and Air Jamaica.

We helped Omnipoint, a start-up wireless company, grow and become T-Mobile.

We launched Pasta and Cheese pastas and sauces which, in turn, launched the fresh pasta and sauce industry.

More gratifying than any of these, we had a profound effect on the issue of domestic violence in America. This is the one thing I'm most proud of.

We won multiple awards along the way and became one of the more admired creative agencies of its time. The idea that, from these tortured beginnings, we could become a credible agency is incredible.

The rest of this book will be dedicated to a detailed account of events that happened along the way at Altschiller Reitzfeld. Most of the stories are funny; a few of them sad. They recount the day-to-day insanity that goes on in the business. All are true. In some cases, where the occurrences are hurtful to individuals, or might provoke lawsuits, I've changed the names of the guilty. (But not often.)

I won't argue that these stories were everyday events. Some are so improbable, it's hard to imagine they ever happened at all—but they did.

The Poop Man

WHEN you're a small agency and just starting out, clients show up who wouldn't normally dare set foot at established places. People with failing businesses and half-baked ideas somehow smell you out. I guess they figure you're in as much trouble as they are, and sadly, they're right. I remember one particularly silly one...

Weeks after the agency opened its doors, New York City passed a poop law. Do you remember it? It said you had to pick up after your pup or be subject to fine.

Suddenly, the streets were filled with bent over people with plastic bags on their hands. New York was becoming the picture of a world of butts pointing to the sky picking up poop. This was not quite sunbathers picking up shells on the beaches of Seychelles.

About a month after the poop law changed the life of New York dog owners, a man showed up at our office unannounced. He was a Brit, as I recall, and quite elegant. That's how he got past Florence, our mother-office manager-protector.

In short, the Brit had invented something to take advantage of New York's crappy problem. I promise you he would have not shown up at a credible agency like BBDO.

Of course, we met with him. At that moment, we'd meet with anybody.

He explained in his Oxford accent that it was not seemly to pick up poop from the street with your hand. Oh? Really? And he had invented something that would cash in on this messy situation.

He then pulled his invention from one pocket and a wrapped handful of poo from the other. Suddenly, he unwrapped the nugget and dropped it naked on the rug. We were wide-eyed, to say the least. What was this lunatic doing on the agency's only rug?

The invention was in a spray can. He leaned over, pressed the top of the spray can, and a stream of bright, blue goop resembling Marshmallow Fluff was expelled and engulfed the poop. Ten seconds later, the poop had hardened into a solid blue mass. Without hesitation, he picked up the volcanic pile and stuffed it into his pocket.

This was clearly not the IBM account. This was actual poop, and it was indicative of where the agency was at this moment. If we promoted his invention, we'd become known as the poop group. (Well, at least we would have been known for something.) So, we politely turned down his business. But we graciously gave him a name for it free of charge: "Wrap Shitty in Blue." It even came with its own melody, but obtaining the Gershwin rights would have been a bear.

The Return of NCK

IN the months after the poop man, the agency began picking up larger pieces of business. Not large — larger. We had established a good creative reputation and were on a roll. Kind of a mini roll. Then, out of the blue came something that would change the direction of the agency for some time.

We received a call from NCK Worldwide based in Europe. Remember them? NCK was the awful, first real copywriting job I had. The one with Norman B. Norman? Well, the Europeans told us they were interested in buying our agency. Not only that, but they'd like us to take over running all their business in the United States and manage their American headquarters, Norman, Craig, and Kummel, New York.

Is this a made for TV movie or what? They were willing to pay big bucks for us to run the agency where I had started my career, pathetically so, a little more than a decade before. This seemed to be an incredible opportunity. Not only did they want us to roll our fledgling accounts into this big-time television behemoth, but we were asked to take over their roster of world-class clients: Revlon, Chanel, Colgate-Palmolive, Maidenform, Jeep, and others. Of course, we had to forget the fact that many of these clients had been creating pedestrian work compared to the work we were now doing at our agency. But we would change all of that for them. After all, the only reason their work was so forgettable was that it was missing our brilliance. Proof that you are never too young (or too old) to be arrogant.

When we received that call from NCK, however, we were missing an important piece of information. While NCK Worldwide had grown into a huge, international advertising empire, the

American agency we were about to take over had been secretly crumbling. ("Secretly" being the key word here.)

After we made the deal with the Worldwide Group, (emphasis on "after"), we learned that Mr. Norman B. Norman had already lost much of the agency business. We had been told that Norman was retiring, not that the Europeans had "retired" him.

Now, we were supposed to unravel the mess. How this information could have been hidden from the world — and more important from us — is bewildering.

As our first exercise after making the deal, and lining our pockets, we moved into the lavish NCK top floor offices on East 55th street. These were the offices where they shot *Kramer vs. Kramer*, with views from the Hudson to JFK airport. Immediately, we began to visit every notable client. In each case, we were told the same story: the client wanted no part of NCK or us and there was nothing we could do to change that decision. At some point, bad stuff had gone down and they didn't care who we were or what great commercials we had done. The boat had sailed, the dye was cast, and any relationship with NCK was kaput. "Nice meeting you!" This was a chilling and bewildering series of events.

The notion that Norman and the entire New York management team had kept this poisonous fact from their European partners is beyond understanding. Or did they? Was this a giant U.S./European conspiracy? Were they either notorious liars or world-class fools or both? To this day, I don't know. But, the simple fact is, the Worldwide Group ended up paying my agency a big pot of money for us to manage nothing.

Or was there is another version of the story? Did the Worldwide Group know NCK New York was in trouble and, in desperation, reached out to us hoping our stellar creative reputation would hold their notable clients in place? They withheld this information from us knowing that if we discovered it, we'd wouldn't make the deal. To this day, decades later, I still have no clear idea as to the truth of the situation. One thing I knew: the deal was predicated on taking on a roster of world-class clients and now it was devoid of those clients.

Could we get out of the deal? Having made it, and taken the money, was there any going back? Could we announce that this big merger, which just days ago had been splashed all over the newspapers, was a colossal mistake? We would become enmeshed in a major industry public relations disaster. All we could do is make the best of it. All we could do was begin to focus on our new agency, no bigger than our old one, now carrying a big agency name and big agency headaches.

It is important to understand, we had not made the NCK deal for the money. We made it to give ourselves, and our employees, a jump-start to becoming a serious and enormous agency; to do great work for world-class clients with world-wide visibility. They served up a big lie, and we ate it up.

Rather than growing our little agency, we had to de-populate the big agency we were suddenly running. You see, before we arrived, NCK management hadn't had the courage, or the decency, to let go of all the employees who no longer had accounts to work on. NCK asked us to wield that ax. First, no clients. Now, the opportunity to be mass murderers.

In the weeks following, we had to fire close to 100 people. People we didn't even know. It was the most painful thing any of us had ever done. We became the executioner in a war we never fought. If you've never been part of a mass firing, there is something surreal about it. Employees wait anxiously in their offices to find whether they would be saved or discarded. Some angry, some bewildered. In the end, few saved.

Understanding the economics of the agency business does not require a doctorate. Clients pay you fees or commissions, and from these you have two major expenses: rent and salaries. If your income exceeds its expenses by a lot, you get rich. If your expenses exceed your income, after not too long, you're out of business. It's as simple as that.

Anyone who has ever rented space knows that leases are difficult to break. You are allowed to get out of them only if you pay big penalties.

Cutting salaries is easy, you just fire people. You simply ruin people's lives. I say this bluntly and cruelly, because there is nothing crueler than making a person pay a price for a thing they were not responsible for in any way.

This was a mind-numbingly painful and disruptive time.

For about a year after the bloodbath, the the agency was growing and normalizing. Then something miraculous happened.

In the same way that NCK came out of the blue to buy us, they came out of the blue to ask to part ways with us.

NCK needed a big presence in the U.S. to match their world-wide business. Without all the huge accounts that had left NCK in New York, our stand-alone, small agency was not a world-class alternative. The idea, I guess, was that our creative reputation would retain those clients. Not a chance.

So, in an effort to dramatically enlarge their lost business base in America, the Worldwide Group engineered a merger with another giant U. S. agency: FCB.

There was one problem: we stood smack in the way of the deal. When we were negotiating our contract with NCK, we had a stroke of genius that we never thought we would ever need to use. We demanded that they include a clause that said we would be the only NCK agency in the U.S. They agreed to this because they didn't expect they'd need one at the time. But they sure did now.

Tough luck, guys. You can't merge with anybody.

We had NCK over a very big barrel. They had to make this deal with FCB. After negotiating with NCK, in return for allowing them to enter into their new merger, we were able to keep all the money they'd paid us and have our agency back for free! What an unexpected turn of events. We were dancing, not simply because we got money for nothing, but because we were out of this nightmare.

There is one last, dramatic ending to this story. Maybe the last scene in the movie — like *Rosebud*. (This whole NCK fiasco could be a movie.)

One evening, at the very end of the NCK saga, I was working in my office late in the evening. From the corner of my eye, I saw several moving men enter the office of Norman B. Norman. (As a courtesy, NCK Worldwide had allowed Norman to keep his office after we took over the agency. Over the months, he never uttered a word to us, nor we to him. It must have been very uncomfortable for him. It sure was for us.)

On this evening, NCK Worldwide undid the courtesy. The movers walked into Norman's office and removed his desk — with him clinging to it. He walked beside his desk, down the long hall, one hand clutching the desktop, and past all the empty offices of his fired employees. (Can't you see the ghosts coming out of their offices shaking their fists at him?) He entered the freight elevator still holding onto his desk. I never saw him again. Terribly sad, almost Shakespearean—great men falling from great heights. Except Norman was no great man.

Mae West

ONE of the amazing things about the ad business is that you never know what's going to come through the door or who's going to be on the other end of the phone.

One day, out of the blue, I get a call from Mae West. (Well, actually Mae West's agent.) He tells me that Ms. West has great affection for our client Poland Spring's famous water. In fact, she bathes in it.

Now, I had no idea that Mae West was still alive, no less playing with her soaky toy in Poland Spring.

"Err... Ms. West is still with us?" I ask.

"She sure is, and in fine health."

I hesitate.

"How old is she now?" I inquire.

"David, we never discuss things like age," he replies.

I imagine Mae West was close to 90. I also imagine that the agent is calling to score a lifetime supply of Poland Spring. Which, at her age won't be much. I also realize that the story of this legendary star bathing every day in Poland Spring water might be a terrific radio commercial.

The agent says, "For the right price, you know, she might even read a spot for you."

"Really?" I say, and add—with some trepidation, "Can she still... act?"

"Sir, this is Mae West you're talking about. She is the consummate professional." I ask him in several other ways whether her performance is still what it was.

He replies that she is not the least bit diminished.

I think to myself, *"Well, if she can still perform, and if we can get her inexpensively enough, there's a lot of upside."*

I write four radio spots for Ms. West. She approves them and I fly off to Hollywood to record her. I'm waiting outside the recording studio when a very long white limousine pulls up.

Handlers run and open the door. The first thing I see is two tiny feet in 4 in. high, white, platform shoes followed by a very small being in white. In the 4 in. shoes, she can be no more than 4 ft., 9 in. tall. In her hay day, maybe she was five feet. When she famously said, "Is that a pistol in your pocket or are you just happy to see me?" I think she was eye-level with the pocket. Funny, I always thought of her as a big woman. I thought wrong.

Along with her comes her weight-lifter companion. I think she's always had a weight-lifter companion. This one is about 80 years old.

We lead Ms. West slowly into the recording booth and off we go.

Now, when you're shooting television commercials, the agency hires a director to direct the talent and a production company to produce the spot. In radio, the agency hires a recording studio and often the writer acts as the director. I've always loved this, because it's the one opportunity where I could cast the talent myself and arrive at the performance I imagined when I wrote the spot.

But only if I had cast the right talent.

To make a very long story short, the Mae West at the studio was no longer the Mae West I'd remembered. When she opened her mouth, I expected to hear the "come up and see me sometime" voice.

Instead, I was hearing some old lady.

"Oh, you want me to do the character?'

"No," I thought, *"I flew all the way to California to get a reading from someone who sounds like my Aunt Bee."*

"Yes," I say, "we'd like you to do the character."

The truth is, I never had any idea that there was a character. I thought Mae West in real life sounded like Mae West.

When Ms. West begins to read, she does fine as Mae West for a couple of sentences and then falls out of character. She keeps doing this. A few sentences of Mae West followed by an unidentifiable older person.

Soon, I find myself doing the one thing you're taught never to do to an actor. I give her line readings.

This is crazy! I am doing my line-by-line impersonation of Mae West to Mae West. And then Mae West is doing my line-by-line impersonation of herself back to me.

At this point, I am sweating from every pore in my body. I soon find myself having to explain the dirty double entendres in the spot to the person who turned dirty double entendres into a career.

We have four commercials to do and I know Miss West, even in her prime, would wilt doing multiple takes of multiple lines. 90-some year old Mae could have a stroke. Even worse, *I* could have a stroke.

I'm trying to gauge how much I can push her before I lose her. For the moment, she's holding up. I decide I'll record three commercials, maybe two.

Then, something completely unexpected happens. In the middle of a sentence, she stops reading abruptly. She makes not a sound. I panic. Did she have a heart attack? I ask her weightlifter to run into the booth to see what's wrong. He comes out and whispers in my ear.

"Ms. West," he says, "doesn't like the word."

"Word? What word?"

"Old... Miss West doesn't say the word 'old' "

Oh, my God! In the spot, I had written, "Poland Spring is like an old friend."

I say to myself, *"What next?"*

"Would Miss West say, 'like a good friend?'" I ask the weightlifter.

"Perfect," he says.

At another abrupt stop, I learn that she's unhappy again.

The script reads "Poland Spring comes in two sizes: small and big. (pause) I prefer big."

Mae West objects to "big." Hey! She got the double entendre! The weightlifter whispers to me, "Ms. West says it's dirty."

Dirty? Of course, its dirty! Am I going crazy? I thought I was writing for Mae West. Am I writing for Billy Graham?

The abrupt stops never stop. My line-by-line impersonations of Mae West are wearing me out. I record two commercials. I don't know how much she can handle. It's certainly all I can handle.

At last, we finish. We wave bye-bye to the really sweet lady in white and head back East with a jumble of usable half-sentences, 2- and 3- and 5-second snippets of tape. The hope is that these clipped utterances will get judiciously spliced together to sound like actual thoughts and end up as a pair of coherent commercials. I'm shaken. This has been the most stressful production experience I've had to date. (Just wait, there will be worse.)

I have low expectations. I am prepared to give the client back his production costs and eat the spots. I'm convinced they will be a herky-jerky disaster that will sound more like a woman with a terrible stutter than one of the great comediennes of all time.

These days, the digital age, editing is fast and electronic. Almost anything can be done. "Can you shave a half second off the spot? Can you cut that pause in half? Can you make that T sound less like a D? Easy... today.

When we recorded these, not all that long ago, editing meant you literally had to cut the recording tape with a razor blade into snippets and scotch tape them together. (In the digital world, this must sound like the dark ages.) In cutting the West spots, there were thousands of 1- and 2-inch pieces of tape everywhere. How our brilliant editor, Bobby DeFranco, could find the right 1-inch piece from among all the others amazes me. The fact that he made the spots coherent and somehow even gave them perfect comedy timing is something that's nothing short of genius. Despite all the pain in recording, the spots sound unlabored and genuinely funny. Mae West sounds exactly like Mae West. Aunt Bee is nowhere to be found. The spots went on air and became an instant sensation. This is the first time anyone has learned the truth of those famous commercials.

As you will hear me say several more times in this book, "Another day, undetected."

Creativity Takes Courage

BRINGING great creative work into existence requires more than talent, it demands guts.

There are thousands of very talented creative people in the industry. Have you noticed thousands of truly creative commercials on TV lately? Hundreds? Dozens? Why is this? So many commercials created, but so few great ones.

Along the way somebody lacked courage. Courage? Yes. Nothing more. Most truly great work never leaves the agency, or if it is lucky enough to be presented to clients, never gets sold.

Before we go down this road, I guess you deserve a simple definition of how I define "exceptional creative work." To me, it is work that has not been done a million times before, work that is not derivative, and the highest hurdle, it is work that makes people see what you're selling in an entirely new way.

With that as a given, exceptional creative work is hard to create and even harder to sell.

How does an agency justify asking a client to spend a lot of time and money to sail into unchartered waters? What does it take to attempt to accomplish something that hasn't been successfully accomplished by others before? How does a marketing person decide to put his job at risk by championing something unproven?

To minimize risk, big clients employ all sorts of consumer research, focus groups, plus qualitative and quantitative testing. But all this is done after a campaign is presented, not before. Before money is spent to underwrite the work, the client has to see — and approve — the commercial idea.

This means the agency has to take a risk without some mythical, foolproof assurance that the client won't view it as a mistake. Risk makes some agencies very afraid.

Here's an ugly story on the subject:

We once had a partner who did a truly unforgiveable thing. (The story is so ugly; I won't use his real name. Let's call him "Larry.")

Larry, as our marketing partner, was not only supposed to be the person most responsible for the strategy behind the creative work, but he was the chief liaison with the client and the person who was supposed to support the work in marketing terms and help sell it. One day, as part of the intra-agency process, Bob Reitzfeld and I showed Larry work we were about to present.

In the package of work we showed Larry, there were several commercials the client could have bought with little difficulty; commercials right down the middle of the marketing plate. And there were—as was our way—several commercials that pushed the envelope.

We were not stupid. We knew what the client was likely to buy, but we always felt that what was also required of us, in every presentation, was to present work that was a stretch for him; something truly unexpected. We always believed that if an agency can't offer a more creative vision than the client has preconceived, the client might as well do the work himself.

Unfortunately, as was made very clear by subsequent events, Larry did not share this point of view. To him, "If it isn't a layup, don't attempt the shot." Work that was a stretch scared the crap out of him. He concluded that if the client simply saw this more creative (and better) work, it would lead him to believe we did not understand his business and he would summarily fire us. In truth, the work we presented demonstrated we completely understood the client's business. At our internal meeting, Larry simply nodded at it.

Then, Larry did the unpardonable. After meeting with us, Larry called the client—behind our backs—and told him that the work we were to present later in the day was dangerous and shouldn't be considered. This, from our partner!

How could he commit this supreme act of advertising treason? Simple. He was scared out of his mind.

If I were kind, I'd suggest that he was trying to "save" the agency by proving to the client that there was at least one person at the agency who would act in the client's interests. But truth be told, I think Larry was trying to save his own neck. In his fear, he assumed that the agency would lose the business because of its rashness and at least he could personally retain the client relationship for use at some future date — at some other agency.

End of story: the client called me immediately after Larry's phone call and asked me what was going on. He'd never seen this kind of behavior, either.

What could I tell him? "We have a nervous partner," I laughed. I then spent the better part of an hour assuring our client that the work he was about to see later was not nearly as risky as Larry said it was. Sure enough, when we presented the work later that day, the meeting went well. While he didn't buy the work that was way, way out on a limb, he bought a commercial that our friend, Larry, *thought* was way out enough that it would cost us the business.

The next morning, we said goodbye to Larry. In the previous day's meeting, Larry had stated his case to us and lost. To expose our client to our internal disagreement was disloyal and destructive and would put in question all future creative work we did for, and with, him.

Before I end this story, there's a trick I should tell you about firing someone. Dick Jackson taught it to me, and I promise it works. Firing is the saddest and most difficult thing you have to do in business. But this little trick makes it at least achievable. As soon as the person's ass hits the seat, before you engage in a syllable of small talk, you declare, "Larry, we have to let you go." If you wait, if you begin with unrelated civil conversation, it becomes impossible. Just deliver the bad news first, and then explain why.

By the way, firing our partner the next day was not accomplished without a lot of difficult soul-searching. We believed that several of the accounts at the agency were the result of our partner having established strong relationships with the clients. We were convinced that we might lose some of them as a result of the firing. But it was clear to us that if we allowed the agency to be held hostage by this kind of fear, we might as well close up shop. And, frankly, we thought by firing Larry, closure was a strong possibility. This was a sleepless night.

The truth is, we didn't lose one client. As I gave all our clients the news of our partner's departure, I came to realize that they were there for the work, not for the schmooze. "Oh, Larry's leaving? Well, that's too bad. I liked Larry. When will you be over to show us next year's campaign?"

I was shocked by the lack of negative response. After all my years in the business, I should have understood advertising's reality. I had underestimated the clients. I also had come to believe that they required some sort of interpreter beyond us to buy into the work. This new realization—that our work didn't require someone with two Harvard MBAs to make sense of it—changed the rest of my advertising career.

What you simply had to do to make clients relatively comfortable was make it clear, with faultless logic, that the creative work you were presenting was a direct result of the strategy that had been agreed upon; a far more creative, more memorable, expression of the strategy, but nothing more. If presented properly, the creative solution was the natural and inevitable outgrowth of the plan. In fact, at the beginning of any meeting involving creative execution, we'd begin with reiterating the strategy and then proceed tiny step by tiny step until the execution was clearly the most intelligent solution.

One well-known agency solved this creative puzzle in a demonically simple way.

When the client and the agency arrived at a strategy, the copy in the commercial articulated the abbreviated strategy virtually word for word.

Directly expressing the strategy with a few words of the audio track freed the agency to execute the drama in the spot hilariously without the least bit of confusion. In research, it performed brilliantly! People recalled the message flawlessly. How could they not? All they had to do was repeat the few words they had heard. The words acted as a touchstone to the memorable drama in the commercial.

Perhaps the most famous example of "say the strategy" was created by Cliff Freeman in the 1980s before he started his own agency. In fact, it helped put his agency in business.

I'll give you an example of Freeman's technique: the strategic logic in this Wendy's commercial begins with the line: "Having no choice is no fun" and ends with "having choice is better than none." Simple, huh? We give you choice. What's so memorable about that? The very simply articulated thought is free to be dramatized. Rather than describing all the food choices Wendy's gives you, which would be hopelessly boring, the spot was now able to talk about something more engaging than lettuce and tomatoes—the idea of choice and no choice.

The commercial created a parody of a Russian beauty contest in which an overweight Russian "fashion model" struts the runway in various costumes; promoting daywear in a baggy blue dress, evening wear dressed in the same blue dress now carrying a flashlight, swimwear in the same dress with a beach ball. See? They simply and memorably articulated having no real choice with no communications risk. The client got a very high research score, and the agency got a world-class commercial.

Here's a second, more bizarre story of a client so afraid of risk he wanted to create an exact replica of what had already been famously done.

One day, our agency met a prospect we knew little about. Our new business person had received a call from him and based on the call, arranged a meeting.

After our initial presentation, he quickly hired us. We began having long discussions about his business issues and what he believed was strategically required of the work we'd create. Among other things, he told us he wanted "an Avis campaign."

If you recall, Avis had created a highly publicized campaign against its larger competitor, Hertz. The theme of this notable campaign was "We're number 2. We try harder."

In the advertising business, that campaign was one of the first of a genre of super-competitive ads that directly attacked a competitor by name. Advertisers do that often these days, but back then, this kind of no-holds-barred, head-on corporate warfare was thought of by some as uncivilized and was almost unheard of.

We said to our new client, "The Avis direction sounds great." We loved doing pugnacious advertising. I had done this at Ally for years. So, several weeks later we came back to him with a very aggressive effort that pulled no punches. We were quite proud of it.

Our client sat quite quietly after he saw the work. At last, he said, "So where's the Avis campaign? Where's the 'We're number 2. We try harder'?"

"What do you mean," I said, "This has the same highly competitive spirit as that. What don't you see?"

"It don't see the, 'We're number two. We try harder.'"

Hard to believe, but our new client had actually expected that we'd come back to him with an exact knock-off of one of the most famous campaigns in recent advertising history. I guess you can get away with that kind of thing in the garment industry.

Is the person who makes all those imitation Hermes bags ashamed? Is the man who put the names Emilio Pucci and Guccio Gucci together to create "Emilio Gucci" now in hiding? No. In some industries, every day they take their plagiarism to the bank.

But in advertising, you simply can't be that baldly larcenous. You can't steal a set of words that have been trademarked and have been in such wide usage by a client for so long that they become associated with that client. It is both illegal and morally reprehensible.

While I never heard anyone insist on a trademark invasion before, or since, knock-offs of visual style, or tone of voice, or even advertising claims are requested by clients every day. Stolen ideas are acted upon by agencies all the time. They've seen it done before, and they've seen it perform in the marketplace before — why not steal it?

After three decades creating the Boar's Head work, I can show you dozens of competitor's commercials that stole our visual ideas, our point of view, and even our claims. After all these years, I am still infuriated by it. Imitation may be considered the sincerest form of flattery, but it is also the lazy marketer's most common method of theft.

The sad reality of copyright law is that while you can legally protect exact language, you cannot protect ideas. And even sadder, there's a whole industry of people waiting for you to have an idea they can rip off.

This is especially true of ideas that have proven themselves successful over time, like Boar's Head. Oddly enough, "appropriating" someone else's idea in advertising is most often done by the largest advertisers in a category. Because they have such a large budgetary advantage over their competition, they can take a smaller competitor's idea, put a ton of money behind it, and in short order, own the idea in the public's mind. Happens every day.

Which takes us back to the beginning of this chapter and the idea of fear. Taking someone else's commercial idea which was successful in the marketplace would appear to be great defense against fear. "If it worked for them, why not for us?" It's why you see so many copycat ideas. It's the genre that our old friend Larry most preferred. Unfortunately, experience shows that what worked for somebody else is no guarantee that it will work for you. Yet another thing to fear.

Ray Charles

ONE of the big problems with campaigns that use celebrities is that you remember them but you might not have the foggiest idea of what they were promoting. That's because. very often. the celebrity has no real relationship with the product or with any attribute you'd like people to remember about the product.

"Hey did you see the commercial with Derek Jeter?"

"Yeah."

"Who it was for?"

"Huh?"

We've all seen commercials with football players or tennis players wearing fancy watches. What does the celebrity have to do with the watch? Well, he's wearing it. The assumption is that if you admire Roger Federer, you'll be prepared to plunk down $10,000 so you can be admired for wearing the same watch. It's a stretch as far as I'm concerned.

Of course, if clients have enough money, they may be able to run the commercial often enough so that people will vaguely remember the association of the celebrity with a watch. Which watch? I don't think we can expect that much.

Bob Reitzfeld and I were fortunate enough to create a campaign where the celebrity was intergral with the idea for the campaign. The celebrity's relationship with the idea was so specific that almost no one else on the planet could have starred in it. Well, it wasn't simply good fortune. The *idea* came first, then the celebrity who related to the idea came second. (In most celebrity spots, the celebrity comes first and there's no idea second.)

The campaign was for Pioneer LaserDisc. You may recall, LaserDisc was the first optical disc system — the father of the DVD. It was developed to compete with videotape.

The picture that LaserDisc put on a TV screen was better than what you'd see on TV or videotape. Unfortunately, it was not a *lot* better, but the sound was astounding because LaserDisc was, in fact, the first commercial digital sound system. So, here we had a video system that delivered a marginally better picture than a VCR, but dramatically better sound. How on earth do you sell that?

Well, we conjectured, since the picture isn't so amazing, you have to sell this video system to people who are audiophiles or people whose love is music. So, we created a slogan: "Video for people who really care about audio." We thought it was a good slogan; a line that defines both the product and its audience. But the slogan had a problem. It required a little thought and in a world of 30-second messages and an instantaneous turning of the channel, people actually thinking is not something advertisers can count on.

The question was, how do you make an idea that is cerebral, memorable? In advertising, this is one of the most difficult questions to answer. Could we ever have this slogan make instant sense? Or would we leave our audience scratching their heads?

We began to ask ourselves more questions: First, who cares about music? Everyone. So, that didn't help. Alright, second, is there anyone who might value music *more* than most people? Well, composers and musicians. OK. What about using a musician in the commercial? Makes sense.

Then came the creative leap and I mean *leap*. What about using a person who can only appreciate the audio? What about someone whose audio judgment is not complicated by pictures? What about a blind musician?

Wow.

Dare we consider it? Dare we use a blind musician by highlighting his blindness? Could we possibly get it on the air? In this era of social correctness, we quickly concluded — not in a million years. The Association for the Blind would march on the agency. Worse yet, all those millions of social correctness freaks would tsk-tsk us out of business — not just with our client, but our agency.

That was our first thought: It's a great idea, but we can't do it. We were on the verge of abandoning it, but then we had another thought: what if we weren't talking about the blind person in the third person. What if the blind musician was talking about himself? Making fun of his own affliction? If he's not offended by the subject, why on earth should the audience be?

What if this blind musician said, "Music video? I can't see it. If it don't sound good, who cares what the picture looks like." The script almost wrote itself.

Was it scary? Sure, it was scary. Blind people might be offended. People who think blind people might be offended could be offended. This could get ugly. Not that it *should,* but it *could.* We might find the agency picketed by seeing-eye dogs.

I remember several years earlier, we created a TV spot for WYNY, a radio station in New York that played pop hits. The commercial we created starred regular folks singing along badly to famous pop songs. One of the many people, a Japanese fellow, was singing along with Stevie Wonder's voice, "*You are the sunshine of my life, you're the apple of my eye....*" The spot goes on the air and next thing you know, we have hundreds of Japanese picketing outside the agency. They're outraged that we're making fun of Japanese eyes. Can you imagine? It's as if entire populations live their lives waiting to be offended by something.

Over the years, there's one thing I had learned about truly breakthrough work: It's almost always scary. In fact, if you take the time to look back at the best commercials through history, you'll find that the riskier they are, the more memorable they are.

The little girl picking petals off a daisy while the atomic bomb goes off may be the most famous political commercial ever made. This Lyndon Johnson anti-Goldwater spot created by DDB was so scary it almost didn't get out of the agency and when it did, it ran only once. But many people credit it with winning Johnson the election. (Look it up on YouTube.)

Do you remember the introductory Apple commercial called "1984"? It introduced Macintosh. After 55 seconds of high drama and no announcer to explain the action, you didn't quite know what was going on. There was not a product or product name seen or heard. Finally, at the last possible moment, after all this surrealistic and militaristic imagery, suddenly, type comes across the screen, (Not even a voice over, just type) and says, "On January 24th, Apple Computer will introduce Macintosh. And you'll see why 1984 won't be like '1984.'" It had never been done before. No commercial had created so long a dramatic set up for so short a payoff. Never in a commercial was there so much bewildering imagery with virtually no explanation until the very end. And even that all-type explanation was kind of opaque. Scary. The Steve Jobs book tells us the CEO and the Board of Apple were terrified. Somehow, it ran. But it ran just once during the Super Bowl, but once was enough. It put Macintosh on the map. If you're interested in more detail, read Walter Issacson's book on Steve Jobs or find the spot on YouTube.

Now, I won't suggest that the Pioneer spot ever became as famous or iconic as the Apple spot, (it did become famous,) but to those of us who'd created it, it was every bit as scary.

The question was: How could we take some of the fear away?

Here we are with this blind musician idea, but it's still in trouble. We knew it couldn't be just any blind musician. Oh no.It would have to be a really, really celebrated blind musician. Someone whose name alone would bring credibility to the concept. Which one? Well, there aren't too many very, very famous blind musicians to choose from. Ray Charles and Stevie Wonder come to mind immediately! Great. We get Ray Charles and Stevie Wonder to goof on their own blindness, in a TV spot no less. Good idea, but fat chance of getting them.

But we had a wild card up our sleeve: an impossibly fearless account guy at the agency named Howard Mandel. We said to Howard, "We want you to track down Ray Charles' and Stevie Wonder's managers and get them to talk Ray and Stevie into doing the spot."

Most account guys would have looked at us like we were nuts. These were two of the most famous performers in the world. There wasn't enough money in the world to get them, and even then, chances are they wouldn't do it. But Howard was utterly fearless. There was nothing he wouldn't do and no one he wouldn't approach.

He took the idea to Ray Charles' manager, Joe Adams, who took it to Ray and amazingly Ray bought it. Ray thought it was smart and funny, and he wasn't offended by making fun of his own blindness — he was tickled. It must have been some selling job, or Ray was one of the hippest guys who ever lived. But you knew that. One celebrity down, one to go.

Stevie Wonder was a very different story. He didn't reject the idea. No, in fact, he liked it. But he didn't want us to write the commercial — he wanted to write it. We considered this for about 10 seconds. This idea was too strong and too complex a concept to risk screwing it up by pandering to Stevie Wonder. So, without too much regret, we said "bye-bye Stevie." (Remembering my writing experience with Bill Cosby didn't help Stevie's chances.)

Ray was in the bag, but we still needed another blind musician. (I guess Ray could have been enough, but there were two written into the spot.) When you think about it, there aren't that many world-famous blind singers or musicians, are there? We needed someone who'd appeal to devotees of a different musical genre than Ray. We got lucky. We found George Shearing, one of the most famous pianists in the history of jazz; a man with real dignity, and like Ray, famously blind. Having Ray to use as leverage, we got George to sign on.

Now came the real challenge: How do we get Pioneer to buy it?

Our principal client, the head of Pioneer in the United States, was a man by the name of Ken Kai. Kenny was legendary in the audio business. He brought Pioneer Audio to America and turned it into one of the first, great Japanese audio brands. He's widely considered the father of the mass audio industry in America. He was exceptionally bright and exceptionally funny.

When we presented the Ray Charles campaign to him, he thought about it a minute, and then was silent for another minute. We thought we were through. He then began to laugh, and the next minute he bought it. I'm not sure whether he was most excited by the concept or by the idea of having Ray Charles represent his brand, but he was delighted. But we were still not out of the woods. Typical of Japanese companies, who are famously collaborative, Ken needed the agreement of all the marketing people in the room.

Fear is a very powerful emotion and, even in the face of Kenny's acceptance, the marketing guys had their hackles up. Fact is, they were frightened out of their minds. "How can we do this? Blind people will be all over us." One after the other, they articulated all the fears that we had feared.

I was distraught at their response. After all this work, we hit the wall that I always knew in my heart we'd hit. Kenny looked over at me in the meeting and saw my shattered expression. He leaned over and whispered in my ear, "Don't worry, David, I'll call you tomorrow."

What on earth could Kenny do to save our campaign from oblivion?

We thought the idea was brilliant from the beginning and therefore, expected its death at every turn. (Creative people always believe in their hearts that the better a commercial is, the more likely it will be killed.) If Kenny was a martinet, he could have overruled the marketing guys. But this was a Japanese company, consensus and collaboration were the rules of the game.

True to his word, the next morning, Kenny called and said, "I'd like you to meet me tomorrow night for dinner — and bring the script."

"OK," I said. I didn't ask why, but I knew Kenny had something up his sleeve.

When I arrived at dinner the next evening, Kenny and his lawyer were there with the marketing team who had rejected the spot. After an unusually long stretch of small talk, Kenny casually turned to me,

"David, do you have the script you presented to us yesterday? Why don't you read it to our lawyer?"

So, I read the script to the lawyer. I waited for the lawyerly response assessing risk. I couldn't have been more wrong. He was off-the-walls blown away. "This is pure genius, David. Congratulations. Blind musician," he roared, "Brilliant." Effusive doesn't begin to describe his response. Had Kenny rehearsed the lawyer in his lengthy, laudatory response? There is no doubt in my mind.

What was the marketing group to say? Given the lawyer's unrestrained response, they had been trumped. The Pioneer lawyer, the man who is in charge of managing risk, loves it. Kenny is a genius. I've never seen a ploy executed like this before or since.

We were on our way.

On to Ray Charles and the production. The entire experience of working with him was truly memorable. In fact, before we ever got on a set, it proved magical.

Ray invited us to see him perform the next week at The Blue Note, one of the legendary jazz spots in the Greenwich Village. The Blue Note is a small venue with maybe 200 seats. Ray's manager had procured a table that abutted the stage. The stage was about 3 ft. above the audience, and we were maybe 5 ft. away from Ray at the piano. We were practically in Ray's face. Had Ray been sighted, this would have been much, much too close.

Ray began the set with a few words, and then suddenly, in mid-sentence, he began to sing and something otherworldly happened. When he stopped talking to us and opened his mouth to sing, it was as if the sound had not originated with Ray but had come up from the floor and then through him. There was Ray, the person, and Ray, the singer, and they were two different people inhabiting the same body. I'd always believed that this genius level of talent was a gift from God, and the recipient was only a conduit. Now, I was actually experiencing it.

It happened again when we shot the print portion of the campaign. Norman Seiff, one of the great American portrait photographers, shot it. His method with Ray was simple. He put Ray at a piano, and had him talk and play, asking him lots of questions and shooting the hell out of him. By distracting him with conversation he achieved a level of visual candor that would have been impossible if Ray were simply posing stiffly.

Seiff also videotaped the session, and when Ray launched into song to illustrate something, the otherworldliness of his talent emerged again. Ray changed right before your eyes. You can see it for yourself. Part of this now legendary photo session is included in Ray's DVD, *Genius Loves Company*. Watch the DVD and see if I'm exaggerating. The photo session became so famous and so successful that one of the photos from the session is the picture on his obituary.

George Shearing was a lovely addition to the commercial. Certainly, a second banana, but what a charming banana. I spent much of the day, while the director was lighting or Ray was in makeup, with George. He was not simply an exceptional piano player; he was an even more exceptional person.

The chance to work with Ray and George remain unforgettable to me. I didn't know what to expect of Ray's performance. After all, he's a singer, not an actor. But on camera, he was as natural as can be. Unlike Mae West, whose character was different from her person, Ray was Ray, and joyfully comfortable in his own skin. Off camera, he was completely available, regaling us with stories from his life.

End of story: the campaign became iconic. LaserDisc gained instant awareness. Even years later the Ray posters from that shoot can be found in recording studios all around New York. LaserDisc was off to a brilliant start—until DVDs came along and made LaserDisc obsolete.

Liz Claiborne

FROM the beginning, my agency's creative point of view on advertising was based upon two premises:

1. Find a *real* reason for people to buy your product over the competition. There's nothing new here. This has been the classic way people have advertised and sold products since the beginning.
2. Find something to say that's compellingly emotional that will change the relationship between the audience and the product and cause them to see the product in a new way; a way that will separate it from the competition. This direction was often quite effective for us.

When we were awarded the Liz Claiborne Fragrance business, it was evident that there was no substantial reason we could give women to buy it. Fragrance, by its very nature, is ephemeral. It's about scent and seduction. Goodbye premise #1. All that was left was to find some emotional road we could travel.

As we thought about Liz Claiborne, both the person and the company, we had something unique to hold onto: Liz.

Liz Claiborne, the person, was very much the spirit of the new woman. Smart, confident, and living comfortably in the man's world that she was changing. Her clothing had liberated working women from the constraints of "dressing for business." Women were finally free to dress as women. Liz became an icon of women's new fashion freedom.

On the other hand, as we thought about the world of fragrance advertising, what we saw was a vision mired solidly in the past.

The function of a fragrance was not about women feeling good about themselves, but about women being seductive to men.

When Revlon advertised, "Wear it and be wonderful," the "being wonderful" was singularly directed at one's attractiveness to men. Just dab it on and ride a horse into the sunset with Mr. Gorgeous. Don't wear it and you're doomed to a solitary life with no man to comfort you.

Fragrance companies had never considered that women might be wonderful without their expensive stink. Or that they might want to be wonderful for themselves or — heaven forbid — for other women. The premise was that you need this fragrance because, on your own, you are at best not attractive enough, or at worst, utterly unattractive. And this little bit of scent magic will transform you.

As we began to consider the two pieces of the puzzle — Liz's view of women, and the fragrance industry's view of women — we found a powerful place for Liz Claiborne fragrances to live.

Our agency's Roz Greene and her art director partner, Steve Mitch, created a campaign that turned fragrance advertising on its head.

Roz wrote a line that is brilliantly simple and emotionally explosive. The line: "All you have to be is you." So simple. You don't — and shouldn't — aspire to be some fabricated version of yourself. You are enough. Who would think that this quiet revelation could be so emotionally explosive? Yet. it was. It expressed a counter argument to what women had been fed by advertisers all these years: they weren't enough on their own and the product, whatever it was, would fix them. What a relief to be told that you are enough and that you can be yourself without wanting.

Steve visualized portraits of real women just being themselves. The women were shot by Annie Liebowitz as only she can shoot them. Some portraits were reflective, some delighted, all were candid, and very personal.

"All you have to be is you." Just the line, the portrait, and a very small image of the fragrance on the page.

The black and white ad ran in magazines and women ran to stores. Was the fragrance itself so profoundly different that it created this firestorm of response? Not at all. It was the message that was profoundly different. Overnight it became the most successful fragrance introduction in memory. The Fragrance Foundation named it the best campaign of the year.

That night, at the industry's awards dinner, I saw a room full of women stand and cheer for the campaign. The campaign articulated something that women had been waiting to hear, something they'd hoped for even more deeply than the arrival of Mr. Gorgeous: "All you have to be is you." Sales of the fragrance were overwhelming.

But for all its sales and advertising success, the campaign didn't change the fragrance industry's well-worn promises. Sex-driven and fantasy-driven imagery is still pervasive. This is true, I suspect, because the fragrance industry continues to be led by men.

Liz Claiborne (the fragrance) was the first paid advertising campaign the company had ever run. All Liz advertising before this was co-op with retailers. As a result of the success of this first Liz fragrance, the agency was awarded a second fragrance. The company suddenly believed in advertising.

Creating this second fragrance brand was more difficult than the first. The first fragrance relied on an insight. Its power derived from the rejection of the advertising stereotypes.

The new fragrance had to express a fresh insight that would not contradict the first, yet still be different from it. In advertising, you can't do the same trick twice. So how do you start from the same emotional place, and come up with something new?

The foil this time was a fantasy that had been fed to women relentlessly. Somehow, a man on a white horse will appear in your life, sweep you off your feet, and take you to a world far less mundane than the one in which you exist. Wear this fragrance and you will suddenly be so seductive that everyday life will change for you. As the Revlon slogan of years earlier intoned, "Wear it and be wonderful."

If one abiding premise in the fragrance industry was, "you are not enough," the other was, "the life you are living is not enough." Obviously, this fragrance will make for a much more glamorous and exciting existence. Yours will be a life filled with adventure and romance. It will be devoid of groceries, crying babies, incessant trips to soccer games, or frozen dinners.

So, we had another set of fantasies to debunk: a false sense of what living life is really like. .

We named the fragrance: "Realities."

The Realities ads depicted women in down-to-earth, seemingly pedestrian situations, simply being themselves. Uplifting, but always touched with life as it is.

The tag line, coming from the same emotional place as the original Liz fragrance, "Reality is the best fantasy of all." In other words, your life doesn't need to be some fairytale drama. In its everydayness, life *as it is* can be wonderful.

The ad, shot by the brilliant photographer, Pamela Hanson, showed a mother in the bathtub with her one year old, bandy-legged child standing outside the tub and holding on to it, complete with bare bottom. The husband is sitting on the closed toilet next to the tub. This is a situation that could happen on any night, in any household. Seen through the lens of everyday moments, it is magical. The quality of one's life is ultimately measured by the lens through which you see it.

A real-life highlight... The Director of Marketing at Waterford Crystal saw one of the Realities ads in a magazine. Based on the ad, she sought out our agency and hired us. That client, Nina Lyons, is now my wife, and has been for the last 25 years.

Life is Good

SEVERAL years after our series of successes for Liz Claiborne fragrances, they decided to embrace advertising on a broader scale.

For the first time, Claiborne agreed to create image advertising for their multiple lines of clothing products.

Let me explain.

Before the fragrance advertising, the only consistent advertising Claiborne had done was newspaper "co-op," retail-driven ads that partnered with department stores. There had been no "fashion-driven" ads for the brand like the kind you'd see in Vogue or the other fashion publications. The success of the fragrance ads had changed their once purely retail-driven advertising orientation.

But there was something else that made the ads different. If you look at fashion advertisements, even today, they have one thing in common: a depiction of the garment itself and nothing more. Whether its Armani, or Prada, or Gucci, or the lowest of the low end, the merchandise is the star. There is rarely any headline. There's only a fashion photo of the "merch" and the brand's logo.

Liz's ads would become a marked exception. When we began to advertise their fashions, there was always a humorous, ironic headline along with the photo; a different one for each ad. Headlines had distinguished their fragrances, why not make it characteristic of the ads for the clothing as well?

The campaign went on for several years. The headlines were clever and understated. Each one was charged with articulating Liz's attitude not simply about fashion, but about life and her view of the world whether the visual was about shoes, or sportswear, or accessories, or whatever.

Up until this point, while Wendy Banks was our day-to-day client, (and a wonderful one), our ultimate client was Liz herself. She signed off on every ad, and while I never saw her dominate a meeting, I knew if she had the slightest hesitation about something, then that something went nowhere.

Liz was unique. I've worked with many entrepreneurs over the years, but I never experienced someone who exercised more power in a more understated way. Unlike so many heads of companies, I never saw her give the impression that, "Mine is the only vote that counts here."

At the top of the Claiborne company, from the beginning, there were three partners I knew about. There was Liz, her husband, Art Ortenberg, and Jerry Chazen. Liz was in charge of the fashion, Art oversaw production, and Jerry managed sales.

In 1989, the unthinkable happened: there was a parting of the ways between the three of them. I can only guess what it was about, but it was a bad enough disagreement that two of the founding partners, Liz and Art, left the company. This was dizzying for those who remained. For years after, when a decision needed to be made, someone would always ask, "What would Liz say? What would Liz do?" Liz had always been not simply the titular head, but the vision of the company. She was its moral center.

Jerry Chazen was now in charge. And while Jerry was a good man and a strong manager, he was a businessman. Suffice it to say, his orientation was mercantile, not creative. In short, from a creative point of view, he was no Liz.

With Liz and Art gone, Jerry wanted to put his stamp on the advertising, and we were charged with making the change. (I've since felt we should have left with Liz and Art, because it was all downhill from there. But there was a lot of money in continuing with the account, and it was not terrible, just not nearly as good as it had been.)

In the case of creating, "Jerry's campaign" we decided that rather than writing a series of headlines that related to each visual as we had done before, we'd create a campaign with one overarching slogan that would be representative of the "Liz World View."

We envisioned a different woman in each ad. What they all had in common was their unmitigated sense of joy. Sometimes the emotion was subtle, sometimes it was sly, sometimes shy, and sometimes laugh-out loud. These were women who were living in, and loving, the moment.

I was delighted with the campaign. To me, it expressed an uplifting emotion that I felt people needed. So much of life is colored by the attitude you bring to it, and I felt this joyful, positive point of view was useful to all of us. (Somewhere else in this book, I will discuss my strong feeling that advertising's unrealized worth is in the positive values it can add to society. But that's a longer discussion.)

Anyway, I make this impassioned presentation to Jerry. Before I show him the ads, I show him a series of photos of these delighted and delightful women in Liz clothing. Then I say to him, "Jerry, these photos will be unique and stand out in magazines. But they could be anybody's. They are not Liz Claiborne — yet. To become uniquely ours, they need a headline; one single phrase that expresses the Liz Claiborne point of view."

I am buoyed by my own passion. With a burst of enthusiasm and to great fanfare, I deliver my uplifting campaign slogan:

"Life is good."

And Jerry, without hesitation says to me, "You know, David, for many people life is not good."

I'm stunned. For a moment, I don't know what to say. Certainly, life is not roses for everybody, and not for everybody all the time, but "Life is crap," doesn't make much of a slogan.

I fight for the campaign for some time. I try to explain it six ways to Sunday...

"It's important for people to feel positive about life no matter what hand they're dealt," I say.

"Think of all the people in the world in poverty who believe in God."

"Jerry, so much of what brings joy to life is the lens you see it through."

"If you believe life in and of itself is good, you find goodness in it."

"Jerry, this message is important for people to hear."

Jerry is unmoved. The campaign dies in the room.

Nine years later, I'm driving along thinking about nothing and I see a slogan on the spare tire cover of a jeep.

"Life is Good."

Oh, my God. I guess I knew somebody would come to it sooner or later. But on a wheel cover? Well, it didn't stay on the wheel cover long. Today, I see that same slogan everywhere. Even on whole stores featuring "life is good" merchandise.

Clearly, as we had argued years earlier, this was a message people needed to hear.

Every time I see the line these days, it makes me crazy. It would have been a great fashion campaign. And I know that if it were Liz sitting across the desk, rather than Jerry, it would have come into the world. And life wouldn't be as good for the people who belatedly took my slogan.

Domestic Violence

THE most meaningful part of the Liz story was still to come. The principal national organization fighting domestic violence — the Family Violence Prevention Fund — approached Liz to ask for advice in choosing an agency to help change attitudes about domestic violence in this country. She named us, and they hired us.

Along with the work I created for Dr. King's Poor People's Campaign, creating these commercials for them turned out to be one of the proudest achievements of my career.

Esta Soler, the founder of the organization, was a force of nature. In my estimation, she can be credited with leading the change in the understanding of domestic violence in this country. No small feat. She did this with a small organization and a giant heart.

Bob Reitzfeld and I spent a great deal of face time with Esta to gain an understanding of this problem. Domestic violence is a more layered and complex issue than we had imagined. To be successful, we came to realize there were a more than a few attitudes we had to challenge.

The first, and most difficult, misperception was that women were responsible for their own plight. "They drove men to it. Always carping. If only they'd leave the poor guy alone." Inherent in this mindset is that women provoke the problem. Men would not behave badly if women didn't make them crazy.

There were many other rationalizations for abhorrent behavior. Men were not fully responsible for what they did since often they were drunk or drug addled. If they were in their "normal" state, they wouldn't act in this manner.

Then, there was the notion that women commit domestic violence, too. (True, but not nearly in the same numbers.)

And perhaps the most challenging argument: If the men were so bad, why would their women keep going back to them?

Last, the easy throw-away, "It takes two to make an argument."

Beyond this, there was the denial. The public was willing to cross the street, close the blinds, and turn up the sound on the TV in order to ignore what was happening all around them.

"This is their affair."

"It's theirs to work out."

"What goes on behind closed doors is nobody's business."

And the most popular, "We don't want to get involved."

In short, there were an endless list of reasons why this was, to many people, an intractable problem, and why it would be best if everybody would just butt out.

Friends, neighbors, the police, and the courts were, in one way or another, justifying the situation. In short, advertising had to address a myriad of rationalizations.

Rather than joining the chorus, we attacked the problem head on.

Our thought turned into the enduring banner for the movement: *"There's no excuse for domestic violence."*

Impossibly simple. We don't care what your rationalization is, how you explain it, or how you try to justify it; there's no excuse for it. None. There is no way to make it right. No excuse.

If I do say so myself, it was a terrific slogan. Reitzfeld took it further. He created a remarkable graphic. The message was set against a black and blue stripe.

The television advertising posed a difficult problem. Ironically, the networks, an enterprise whose programming mainstay is violence, would not let us show the act of domestic violence in our commercials. "We can make violence part of our daily evening programming, but heavens, not in a commercial," they mumbled. "Unthinkable!"

At first glance, this seemed like daunting conceptual setback, but it proved to be an asset. If we could not show domestic violence in our commercials, we would do something more powerful. We would engage the audience in hearing it. Using the sounds of a couple in an ugly altercation, we allowed viewers to imagine it and in so doing, they became far more emotionally engaged.

You may have seen these commercials. They got a huge amount of airtime. (The media for it was donated by the networks and placed by the Ad Council. This is true for Smoky the Bear and all public service spots.)

In the first commercial, we open on a couple in bed about to go to sleep. She is reading. His eyes are closing. Suddenly, from the apartment upstairs, there's a racket; the unmistakable sound of an escalating domestic dispute. We watch the couple in the bed, jarred by the argument. They both look at the ceiling where the noise is coming from. The wife then looks at the husband. The husband acknowledges his wife's look. There is a moment of indecision. He reaches toward the phone — or so we think. Instead, he reaches past the phone and turns off the light. The screen goes to black, and the title comes up: "It *is* your business." Followed by the tag: "There's no excuse for domestic violence." A simple and, as history would prove, a powerfully indelible message. "It *is* your business," And, for the multitudes watching, perhaps for first time, they were on the hook.

You may not know this, but there's one day of the year that surpasses all others for the commission of domestic violence in the United States — Super Bowl Sunday. People get aroused by the combat on TV, have a few drinks, and let the violence at home begin.

Somehow, we were able to coerce the networks to place the first airing of our commercial during the Super Bowl itself. Quite remarkably, they donated 30 seconds of the most expensive television time of the year to us.

The commercial sent a shockwave across the country and, for the first time, brought the issue of domestic violence to the forefront of the American consciousness. This impossibly uncomfortable subject became the focus of heated discussions on TV talk shows and quiet ones at the dinner table. Of course, it didn't hurt that a few months later, O.J. Simpson, the most publicized person ever for committing domestic violence, was driving in his white bronco on TV screens everywhere. For the first time, the subject of domestic violence was squarely on the radar.

The commercial was given the most prestigious award in the public service sector — Best Public Service campaign of the Year.

The real award, however, was watching domestic violence discussions become part of daily conversation.

After a year of the commercial's airing, and thousands of minutes of donated time, it was time to create another spot.

But how do you follow up on a commercial that broke all viewership records? And given the same restrictions on depicting domestic violence (the networks hadn't relented), how would we accomplish something new while delivering essentially the same message? We found a way.

The commercial opens with a 3 year old standing in the hall outside his bedroom door. Something has brought him out of his room and to the top of the steps. Suddenly, we understand.

We hear an escalating domestic dispute at the bottom of the steps. We do not see the man and woman. The boy walks down a few steps. We see the child seeing the fighting couple. And, as we hear a punch, we watch him recoil as if he were punched. (You should understand, the child's response happened as a result of the director clapping his hands next to his ear, which startled him. He saw no actual violence.)

The commercial ends with the child sitting halfway down the steps, his head between the staircase railings. His expression is somewhere between fear and despair. The look haunts me to this day.

The commercial goes to black and the title comes up:

"He can't do anything. What's your excuse?"

Then a pause, then another title, and the campaign theme: "There's no excuse for domestic violence."

The message, as in the first spot, was an overt rejection of apathy, of rationalization, of standing on the sidelines. It was a true call to action.

For many, this ad was more powerful than the original. The commercial with the couple in bed gave a visual logic to the need for action on the public's part. It attacked the false arguments. It was a caustic comment on doing nothing.

The second spot, as seen from the eyes of a child, is simply heartbreaking. His is not a rational response to the problem. It is pure emotion. We, the viewers, are put on the spot. Are we helpless like the 3 year old, or are we simply content to do nothing? What is our excuse?

Like the first commercial, it elicited enormous public reaction, and once again, multiple awards for public service advertising. Most importantly, it moved the needle once again.

But as I reflect back, I have to face the reality that the issue of domestic violence, while no longer swept under the rug, is far from solved. Society's deeper problems, like domestic violence, racism, and poverty, may be illuminated by advertising, but they will not be quickly changed by it. These will be erased slowly and painfully by relentless efforts of people of good will over time.

A Lesson About the Japanese

KENNY Kai was a wonderful client. He was bright and funny, and admired the work we did. You've got to love a guy like that.

Not long after our success with Ray Charles, I got a call from Kenny.

"David, the Pioneer auto stereo business is up for grabs on the West Coast. Would you like to pitch it?"

"Of course," I said. We already had the Pioneer TV business, so the auto business would help consolidate the account. In addition, we had been told that if we got the auto stereo business, Kenny would take it over and manage it from the East Coast.

The Pioneer client in Los Angeles briefed Kenny, who briefed us, and we began work. Six weeks later, we were in LA making the presentation.

Things did not begin well. The conference room table was filled with 18 Japanese businessmen. We were not sure how many spoke English. Do we speak slowly? Do we speak loudly? Do we assume everyone in the room who looks Japanese was born in the Hollywood Hills?

Our agency's first presenter was a young, eager account person by the name of Howard Mandel. As discussed, Howard had somehow wrangled Ray Charles into doing the commercial for us. Around the office, Howard was known as fearless. But not on this day; he was a nervous wreck. By the time Howard stood on the podium to begin his opening remarks, he had consumed multiple cups of coffee. His shirt was soaked with sweat.

After three sentences, Howard's eyes rolled back in his head and he crumbled to the ground. I thought he was dead. Four of us rushed to the stage. Someone determined he still had a pulse, and we carried him outside the meeting room and laid him out in the hall. We were about to call an ambulance, when Howard's eyes fluttered open. It seems the combination of nerves and coffee had caused him to faint dead away.

But the most bizarre thing was when he collapsed, and all of us jumped up, not one of the Japanese men at the conference table moved a muscle. No one leaped from his seat. As we slowly carried Howard out, no one asked whether they could help, get an ambulance, or do anything.

They just sat there staring blankly at the podium. When we returned a few minutes later to continue the presentation without Howard, they acted as if nothing had happened.

No one asked, "Did he die? Is he on the way to the hospital?" Nothing.

Needless to say, this was not one of our most stellar presentations. The work was good, but the presenters were unfocussed. And why not? One of our band appeared to have died, and the Japanese were oblivious.

I was furious. What kind of monsters were they? I seethed all the way back to New York. First thing back, I called Kenny.

"What kind of people are you, anyway?" I said. I was so angry that I was terribly abusive to this lovely client. "Don't you have any feelings, any compassion? Are you still pissed about the atomic bomb?"

Kenny listened to my rant quietly, then chuckled.

"Oh, David, you understand so little about the Japanese. Of course, we were concerned about Howard, but we could never acknowledge it. To respond to Howard's unfortunate mishap would have been a humiliation for all of you. All we could do was ignore it and allow you to save face."

Over the years, it was one of the many lessons I learned about the Japanese and people in general. Never assume anyone's motives.

By the way, we never got the Pioneer auto stereo business. It seems they liked the presentation a lot, but the account was never really up for grabs. This was a power play on Ken's part to get more control of the account. The account stayed at the agency it always had been. Howard fainted for nothing.

As Carl Ally once told me: "David, it ain't about the work."

Southern Comfort

ADVERTISING research — particularly about the effectiveness of individual print ads or commercials — is not always a reliable tool.

Marketing executives rely on it in order to take themselves off the hook for exercising judgment. If an ad or commercial fails in the marketplace, research is a very convenient place to place blame.

"Hey, I didn't say the ad was good. The research people said it was! They told me the ad was going to work. Here, look at the numbers. I'm not responsible, they are."

Like Hitler's minions, "I was just following orders."

But often research is inexact and even misleading, The main reason for this is that it relies on respondents telling the truth about how they feel. And often, particularly in public, people are notorious liars. Their true feelings can be colored by what they believe the researcher's response will be to their answer, or more broadly, what they think is a socially acceptable response. Is this answer going to reflect well on me? This is particularly true in focus group research when you are responding in front of a room of strangers.

"Will I look dumb?"

"How would others answer?"

"What if I have no opinion?"

"Dare I tell the truth?"

Another reason that research can be wildly inaccurate is it will tell you what people's attitudes have *been*. It cannot tell you what those attitudes *will be*.

How many products and services would not exist today if some entrepreneur had depended upon research rather than his instincts? If he hadn't possessed some overwhelming belief in his own vision in the face of rejection?

But the prevailing attitude among the less entrepreneurial or anti-risk-takers (and these are often the mid-level marketing people), is that while there is some desire to understand the audience's true response, there is an even greater desire to not be responsible for exercising personal judgment about it.

Among some clients, this fear is greater than all others. And much of this fear is derived from how punitive their company will be toward those whose judgment is proven wrong.

Enlightened companies recognize that going down the wrong path is an inevitable step on the road to success. You don't always get it right the first time. But far too many companies are quick to punish unsuccessful decisions with demotions and firings or simply "not thinking well of you." To be succinct, in the marketing business, research results are the defense against personal responsibility. What we have come to know as "CYA" also known as "cover your ass."

All this is a preamble to my experience with Southern Comfort.

The brand was one of several we successfully marketed for Brown-Forman, a huge wine and spirits company in Louisville.

Every idea that Brown-Forman pursued at that time was thoroughly dependent upon research.

When we presented a print ad for Southern Comfort, the ad consisted of a photo and a headline that would be excruciatingly researched beyond all reason.

The photo, however, had not been shot for the ad. Shooting the photo would mean spending money before the idea for the ad was researched and accepted. So we used something the industry calls "scrap." Scrap is an appropriated image that had been shot for another purpose, either as editorial matter for a magazine or for somebody else's ad. If you reproduced it exactly in your ad, that would be outright plagiarism. Scrap was simply meant to provide inspiration for the photo you were about to shoot. By no means was the scrap to be slavishly replicated.

In the days prior to the use of scrap, notably before computers, an art director would simply draw a sketch to represent the photo's intention.

This was not a literal depiction of the intended photo, simply a drawing that the photographer had all sorts of latitude in interpreting.

The sketches were consciously inexact representations, often stick figures. They allowed the photographer to exercise creativity which, after all, was why you paid him so much.

But for some research-dependent marketing people at risk-averse companies, scrap was not meant as inspiration for the photo about to be taken. When the ad was researched, should it be successful, there was little latitude for the photographer's input. The scrap was taken utterly and completely literally.

I recall an instance when we presented the actual photo we had shot for the ad to our client. It was rejected for not conforming to the successfully researched scrap because the man's head was looking to the left rather than the right. Huh? What difference it made to the meaning (or research success) of the ad if the head were looking left or right is beyond me. But heaven knows, if somebody's boss's boss asked why the head was looking left rather than right and he had no answer, it could be *his* head.

Despite this, we were actually able to create some exciting work for the folks at Brown-Forman. (Even though the visual was much too informed by the scrap, the headline was new.) Like the Liz Claiborne ads, the headlines were philosophically in support of enjoying the moment.

"Work, work, work, fish."

"Work for a living. Play for a life."

Beyond the ads for Southern Comfort, we created television advertising for a new product of theirs called Tropical Freezes. These became the most successful of the pre-made frozen cocktails ever. In fact, Tropical Freezes was judged by the American Marketing Association as the most successful new product introduction — of any kind — that year.

How, in the face of the client's research dependency, did we produce memorable and successful work? All I can say is that the ability to create something funny or interesting inside this suffocating research box is much easier to accomplish when you're creating a TV commercial rather than a print ad. (Remember the Russian Beauty contest we discussed earlier?)

Sadly, in the years that have transpired, this submissive dependency on research has grown so much that truly new, non-derivative work is hard to find.

I'm sure you've noticed the sameness. Should someone ask you why there is so little "great work" in commercials or ads these days, you might tell them "Great work cannot be a knock-off" or maybe more telling, "Great work is not created in an atmosphere of great fear."

The Tic Tac Goodbye Party

YOU would think that hiring an agency, with the future of the brand and millions of dollars at stake, would be a well-thought-out, logical decision. You'd think it would be based upon an agency's track record, an analysis of its experience in the category, and perhaps most importantly, the overall quality of its creative work. You'd think.

But very often, the hiring of an agency can be a downright illogical decision, based upon emotional factors which have little or nothing to do with the prior performance of the agency or the excellence of their work. Often, it's about the political dynamics between clients rather than anything on the agency side.

Firing an agency is often more political than logical, as well. I've seen agencies get fired after years of bringing a brand huge sales success. Conversely, I've seen agencies retained after having struck out on a brand for decades. As in hiring, firing is all too often a function of company politics or individual ambition.

Does this sound a little cynical? Let me give you an example.

One day, I'm sitting in my office and out of the blue I get a call from our Tic Tac client. This is not unusual. We've had the Tic Tac account for over a decade and we have created an exceptionally successful campaign and working relationship.

When Tic Tac came to us, they were in more than a little trouble. Several years earlier, they and their huge parent, Ferrero of Turin, Italy, had launched the brand in the United States as an intensely flavored, children's candy. Do you remember, "Put a Tic Tac in your mouth and get a bang out of life."? They had spectacular sales growth. But, as is often the case over time, kids left the franchise for the next candy novelty. You just can't count on the little buggers.

It didn't take long for Tic Tac to plummet from a very success-ful brand to having less than a one percent share of market in the U.S. Their once nationwide distribution had shriveled down to one market: South Florida (That's basically out of business).

The U.S. executives hired our agency at a desperate moment in their corporate lives. Ferrero was a hugely successful, multi-prod-uct company in Europe. If Tic Tac failed in the United States, Ferrero would simply pack their bags and retreat to the Continent.

Why our agency even took on such an ailing brand made little sense. The chance of resuscitating a dying, perhaps already dead, product was a long shot to say the least. Dying brands generally die. However, Tic Tac was a well-known name, and if we could put it back on its feet, it would be a real coup.

Not surprisingly, we recommended that they dramatically change positioning. Not brain surgery, exactly. When the horse you're riding goes lame, it makes sense to get off and change horses.

After a little research, we recommended that Tic Tac give up on selling to children and reposition itself as a breath mint primarily directed to women. Still not brain surgery. Women are the prima-ry users of breath mints. But how could we find a niche in this already crowded and competitive market?

We had a thought: women are quite calorie-conscious and that's why they're eating sugar-free mints. Then we had an in-sight (much better than a thought). We bet that women think that sugar-free means calorie-free. It seemed logical. But the truth is, sugar-free mints have many calories and, good news for us, Tic Tac has just 1½ calories.

Could this insight be consequential? Could a story based upon fewer calories be persuasive enough to women to relaunch a mor-ibund brand? On the surface, it wasn't much to hold on to, but the Tic Tac folks were looking for a miracle. So, they put the question into research. (Boy, did they like research!) The result was unex-pected and off the charts. The research showed that women got re-ally worked up about the fact that they'd been misled — sugar-free *doesn't* mean calorie-free!

You might think this notion wasn't a big deal, but believe it or not, the Tic Tac research numbers broke all the research norms for any commercial tested to that date. Not just for mint-related ads, but for any commercial ever tested! Wahoo! Tic Tac and its new 1½ calorie-driven, sugar-free-debunking advertising was born.

We decided that the commercial needed to be straightforward. Given the overwhelming power of the response from women, we would have been crazy to obscure the message with any sort of artificial drama. This called for kind of stand-up spokesperson spot our agency tried to avoid. (As an agency that constantly aspired to be creative, we much preferred drama and humor to a talking head.) We felt the story was dry and needed humanizing. We did lots of auditions with lots of women. If we were going to do a "stand up commercial", the casting choice, her approachability and believability, would make or break the spot. We selected Kelly Harmon, (sister of Mark Harmon), a beautiful and perky girl next door type who delivered with wide-eyed innocence. She would share something that she had learned that she thought you should know.

"I've got a confession to make," Kelly begins, "I thought that sugar-free meant calorie-free. I was wrong..." She tells the straightforward story with great charm. The commercial ran for years, so maybe you remember it. The fact is, Tic Tac's self-confession sell has been knocked off a number of times by a variety of advertisers. I just saw one on the air with the personal trainer Jillian Michaels, and how does she start the spot: "I've got a confession to make..." People are making more confessions on TV than they make at church.

The Tic Tac success was almost instantaneous and beyond all our expectations. Sales went through the roof. (Considering they had dropped down to next to nothing, "through the roof" wasn't that hard.) For the next 10 years, and multiple TV executions of the 1½ calorie story, Tic Tac saw double-digit sales every year. That's right, double-digit growth every year! For a once dying brand, this kind of consistent growth is unheard of.

So, enough background. Let's get back to this phone call from Tic Tac.

Here we are in year eleven of this multiple-year, ground-breaking success story. The phone rings. The marketing director of Tic Tac asks whether he can come over to see me today at 2:00 p.m.

I say, "Of course."

He calls back an hour later and says, "My boss would like to come with me." I say, "Of course."

I think to myself, *"Uh-oh. Something's going on."*

An hour later he calls and says, "David, can we meet somewhere away from the office?" Bells are now really going off in my head — bad bells.

This can't be good. Why away from the office? But how can it be bad? This is a brand that was in the garbage, that's now no. 1 in the category. Maybe they want to give us all the other brands in the Ferrero stable. I suggest we meet later in the afternoon at the bar of the St. Regis, just a few blocks away from our office. It'll be before 5 o'clock and the place will be empty.

I enter the St. Regis and the place is vacant, as expected. But there's a piano player tinkling away, as unexpected. This is not very office-like.

The three Tic Tac clients come in, and immediately, before any small talk, the marketing director announces that our agency has lost the business. What? This is not possible. This makes no sense.

As if on cue, the piano player begins to play "Music of the Night" the florid theme from *The Phantom of the Opera*. Not even a soap opera could construct this scenario.

I begin to chuckle. This is obviously a joke. Is it April Fool's Day? Somebody's birthday? They even arranged for the piano player. But I see tears come to the marketing director's eyes. I realize this is no joke.

He tells me their parent company wants to launch a world-wide campaign for Tic Tac. He tells me the U.S. campaign, despite its decades-long success, will be abandoned.

I say, "That makes no sense," because *it makes no sense*. He sadly shakes his head in agreement. Quickly, I add "Of course, if anyone's to do a world-wide campaign, it should be us. The Tic Tac success is of our making. Tic Tac has no comparable success anywhere in the world."

"That's true," he says, "but the campaign will be led by the marketing people in Europe and created by Ferrero's world-wide agency, McCann-Erickson." (This is the agency with no comparable success.)

It's clear to me that the Italian parent company wanted to either punish the American marketing outliers or simply take control of the great American marketing miracle themselves.

Could it be that, along the way, American Tic Tac management had become too arrogant for their European bosses? Did they act as if they had done it alone? Had they become self-important? I'll never know. What I did learn is that our television campaign — that won the marketing award as the most effective television advertising campaign in the United States — had come to an abrupt and unceremonious end.

Here's the epilogue:

Almost a year later, a campaign with weirdly European, almost incomprehensible imagery, begins to run. Unsurprisingly, in a matter of months, it's taken off the air.

Months after that, another campaign resembling our initial work, but with a new, younger, less charming version of Kelly Harmon, takes its place. (It takes years to make an actor stand for a brand. They dumped Kelly overnight.) Within months, the "new Kelly" ad is off the air. Here we are, over a decade later, and I've not seen anything on air for Tic Tac since. Nothing!

How could a company snatch defeat out of the jaws of universally regarded victory? How could they walk away from one of the great marketing turnarounds in history? There must be some explanation, but I've never heard it.

In other places in this book, I talk about relationships being the key to keeping clients; not the creativity of the work, not the success of the brand, but building strong relationships with the people who run the business. Unfortunately, while we had wonderful relationships with our Tic Tac clients in America, we came to realize we had forged none with the folks who silently ran the brand from afar — the Italians at the parent company. In hindsight, we should have made it our business to reach out. Would the American marketing team think we were going over their heads? Not if we did it carefully.

Historically, agency-client relationships have a short cycle. In general, things sour after three or four years. We had held on to the Tic Tac relationship for over a decade. No complaints.

Post Cereal

ONE day, we received a call from the Post Cereal division of General Foods. This was very unusual. General Foods was not the kind of large, packaged goods marketer who would seek out a mid-sized, more creative agency like ours. Behemoth clients tend to live at behemoth agencies.

The Post folks told us that their giant agencies, despite numerous attempts, had not been able to come up with a successful new product concept (i.e., a cereal that beat their new product research norms). Therefore, no new Post cereal had come to market for five years.

We were amazed. How could agencies continue to fail for so long and still retain the business? We were surprised at their response:

"Oh, beating our norms is hard," they said.

It was as if Post and the agencies were sitting on the same side of the table and bemoaning their common fate. They were like a dysfunctional marriage—deeply unhappy, but incapable of facing change.

Post told us, however, that they were utterly frustrated and would pay us a huge fee to try to do what their agencies hadn't succeeded at.

We said we'd be happy to take a shot, but not simply for a fee. We reasoned that fees are a one-time thing. We insisted that if we were successful in beating the research norms (which others had so far failed to do) then we would be given the assignment to take the product to market. This would create an on-going income stream for us for an on-going project. We were not willing to be paid a fee—a kind of one night stand—for a product that might succeed in the market for years.

Post said that, despite a 5-year run of failure, they'd never gone outside of their stable of agencies. But, if we were successful, they had no doubt their upper management would agree to make us the agency for these newly created products. With that understanding, with their personal assurances, and with their huge bag of fee money in hand, we proceeded to write ad concepts and positionings and name 11 new products.

The 11 new product ideas were put into their demanding research process. Remarkably, 7 out of 11 beat the norms handily. (Remember, no concept, from any other agency, had beaten their norms for five years prior.) Several of our new product ideas attained research levels not seen by Post before. Why had we beaten their norms the first time out? Why had their existing agencies failed year after year? Were we that good? Were they that bad? Maybe we were fresh and highly motivated. We found this work fun. Maybe they felt stale and defeated.

When our first new product, Post Banana Nut Crunch, came to market, within a year it became a $100 million seller. The American Marketing Association named it Best New Product of the Year. This was no fluke. It was followed by our Post Blueberry Morning and several others. Post was lauded in the press. Our client was touted as a marketing genius.

Did we become the agency for any of these products as we were promised? The short answer: no.

Upper management could not and would not make the change. Did the Post people who hired us for the project ever expect they'd have to approach their top management with our demand that we be their on-going agency? Probably not. I imagine they expected us to fail as other agencies had or, at best, have a middling rate of success.

I imagine you're asking why, with so much unexpected success, would upper management not make the change? Why wouldn't they hire a new agency who had proven they could succeed where their old agencies had consistently failed?

The answer is painfully simple: they were happy with their old agency relationships. Not the work, but the relationships. Somehow, failure had become comfortable in the day-to-day. As long as everybody liked each other, and the client felt like the agencies were trying hard, failure was a sad reality of life.

Although I haven't had the stomach to investigate whether those same agencies are still handling the Post business today, I'd bet they are.

The telling conclusion is that, for many clients, the relationship is everything. If it is pleasant to meet with those other guys, if you like going to work every day, and if you feel respected, you'll accept less from your agency. That is, until someone from above — someone who is outside the relationship — says, "Hey, have you noticed? These guys aren't doing so good!" It explains why, at least at some agencies and with some clients, mediocrity prevails.

It also explains why so many truly creative agencies, who made life less than delightful for their clients, no longer exist.

As referenced before, what Carl Ally once told me in a moment of rare clarity still applies: "David, it ain't about the work."

Pasta and Cheese

POST Cereal wasn't the only instance when major advertising success for the client led to almost nothing for the agency. It's not unusual. I'm sure every agency has multiple stories where they created enormous financial gain for the client and are still waiting to profit from it.

Henry Lambert was an intrepid entrepreneur, a charming and relentless practical joker, and the consummate foodie. While working 9–5 to develop properties for Saul Steinberg's world-class real estate empire, before and after "work," he created and built Lambert's Pasta and Cheese.

Henry is the only wealthy individual I know who had a night job.

When I met with him, Henry had created a handful of retail stores in Manhattan selling the pastas and sauces he had developed in his home kitchen, as well as selling various cheeses that were far superior to what you'd get in your local grocery store.

Henry's neighborhood businesses were growing like crazy in New York. The fresh pastas he offered, the puttanescas, bologneses, and pestos, were priced much higher than Ronzoni in a box or Chef Boyardee in a can, but they were much better.

At this point in history, the idea of fresh pasta was virtually unheard of in American homes. The notion of a fresh sauce, sold in a refrigerated container rather than a can, was equally unknown.

Henry had been prescient about the impending trend towards fast and easily prepared foods. This was not a surprise. While living on the Upper East Side of Manhattan, Henry was surrounded by the rich and time-pressed. His view of the world was colored by those who dined at Lutèce, and La Côte Basque. Price, for them, was of little consequence. In fact, the more expensive something was, the more desirable it was. (Eli Zabar's supermarkets on the Upper East Side built their business on being the priciest. The premise: if it's ridiculously more expensive, it must be better.)

Henry's timing couldn't be better. This was the beginning of a new age. Most women were no longer in the kitchen, nor did they want to be. A new generation of career women had little inclination to putter around fixing something for the hubby or for themselves. The idea of cooking from scratch was fast becoming non-existent. Even men were starting to "cook." This meant that on weeknights, they looked for something to simply warm up. New York had not quite reached the "ordering as a way of life" point yet, but we were on the way.

Henry's idea for fresh pasta that would cook in 5 minutes and a sauce — better than you had ever made at home — that simply had to be heated and poured on the pasta, couldn't be timelier. It was selling very well in his Manhattan retail stores.

But Henry had another and bigger idea. If fresh pastas and sauces could sell in Henry's stores in New York City, why not to families in Westchester? Long island? New Jersey? There was one problem — they'd have to be sold in supermarkets, and that meant they needed advertising to get traction.

In a supermarket filled with hundreds of thousands of items, how would people find them? What's more, what came to be called Lambert's Pasta and Cheese couldn't be sold next to the boxes and cans where pastas and sauces had historically been sold. They had to live in the distinctly un-Italian refrigerated section.

Henry, in perhaps his second most brilliant idea, came to our agency. He had done his homework. He'd watched Altschiller Reitzfeld take Boar's Head from a tiny company supplying ham and bologna to mom-and-pop stores in the boroughs to a national brand that sells at a premium. While Henry didn't have national aspirations, the idea of expanding distribution wasn't a giant leap from Manhattan to Scarsdale, Glen Ridge, and the Hamptons.

Our marketing strategy was simple and logical: make it about taste and quality. Don't even whisper about convenience. Convenience goes arm in arm with compromise. This was going to be about great taste, not lazy preparation. We wrote the slogan early: "Eating in that's as good as eating out." Even those who went to the posh restaurants couldn't dine out *every* night. That was exhausting. Was your only other option to stay home watching TV with a bowl of Cheerios?

Here was the happy alternative. We waxed poetic about the difference between Henry's fresh sauces and the over-processed glop sitting forever in cans. We grew weepy about the difference between pastas made fresh and the dried spaghetti people had grown up with. (We never mentioned the fact that in Italy, dried pasta is used as much as — if not more than — fresh. Which one you use is simply a matter of the dish you're making.) We talked about fresh ingredients and chef-made — not chef-inspired, but painstakingly made — sauces.

By choosing Lambert's, you were not a corner-cutting lazy slug. Henry's solution was far better than what you could make at home. After all, these were chef-made sauces, and who makes their own pasta anymore? Certainly, you'd never cheat yourself or your family for the sake of convenience. Not you!

We followed the Boar's Head advertising model: humorous radio commercials and beautiful posters. In this case, posters on commuter trains, not in New York delis.

The sales result was dizzyingly instantaneous. Products flew off suburban supermarket shelves. Overnight, Lambert's Pasta and Cheese had started a revolution. Was it the brilliant concept? Was it the recipes? Was it the impeccable timing of the product coming to market? Was it the advertising? All, I would suggest.

Henry, flush with success, considered next steps. He offered me a small percentage of the company in appreciation. I began to figure out what I'd do with this windfall. But before my newfound wealth would appear, rumors of an army of competitors appeared on the horizon. Whispers of General Foods, Unilever, and heaven-forbid, Proctor and Gamble's interest in the fresh pasta/fresh sauce category began to appear in the press. Given Henry's success, I guess it was inevitable. But so fast? Maybe we should have expected it. Business is replete with companies that are rich in cash but poverty-stricken in original ideas. They lie in wait for companies to have brilliant visions they can poach.

Henry was panicked. What to do now? He had two choices: raise millions from friends and family to defend his fledgling franchise from the coming giants or sell. "If we raise the money,

David, you'll get a piece of the action. After all, what you created got those companies to the table."

Did Henry raise the money to fund a marketing effort? Nope. Henry sold. It was a much easier route.

Del Monte quickly came along with $56 million. A pretty penny for a less than a year-long marketing effort. After the sale, they didn't even keep Henry's name on the package to cash in on the equity we had built in New York. They took the refrigerated packaging and the formulas and the positioning we had developed and named it Contadina Fresh. Overnight, it was a national brand. And to no one's surprise, it was an instant success. For a short time, they advertised it, but just as quickly stopped. Branded fresh pastas and sauces became a commodity within a year. Del Monte had no more idea how to defend a brand than they had in creating one.

How much of Henry's $56 million did the agency share? We're still waiting. I was disappointed, but not surprised. No one had ever offered the agency anything beyond the commissions and fees it demanded. The way we were paid for success was a piece of bigger advertising budgets. At least in a moment of gratitude and generosity, Henry had offered it. Can't say that of any other client.

Henry and I are friends to this day, and he is still pursuing new food ideas. In support of Henry, I never will eat Contadina Fresh. Poaching is for fish, not ideas.

Joe DiMaggio

THERE are three life-changing things that happened during my years in advertising.

First, I was able to travel to places I never imagined. Better yet, I was able to stay at some of the world's best hotels for long periods of time on somebody else's nickel, and eat truly memorable, stupidly expensive meals.

It is a dreadful admission about business. Because the money spent on advertising efforts is corporate money (and often money from public corporations), it is treated like nobody's money. It gets spent easily and often excessively. These excesses get built into the production company's budgets, which gets billed to agencies at a markup, then billed to clients and ultimately paid by stockholders. The result: It's nobody's money.

I remember spending months at the posh Beverly Hills Hotel while shooting commercials and eating $35 walnut waffles for breakfast. No joke. And this was in the 1970s!

This is one of the major differences between public and privately held companies. In a privately held company, the money is coming out of the owner's pocket and he's saving it for his great-great-grandchildren.

The second great thing about my life as a copywriter: I had new learning experiences every day. Think about it. In most businesses, you do the same thing over and over. You talk to the same vendors, review the same profit & loss statements, argue the same arguments, discuss the same widgets, and deal endlessly with the same marketing dilemmas. Whether you're buying things, or selling things, whether your client is manufacturing things or in the service business; once established, the process rarely changes.

As a creative person in advertising, life was ever-changing. I had to learn multiple different businesses constantly. In fact, I had to learn a different business for every client. The toy business is very different than the supermarket business, the deli business, the fragrance business, the fashion business, the airline business, the automotive business, the fast-food business, or the B-1 bomber business. (Yes, we actually created commercials to market Nothrup's B-1 Stealth bomber to Congress.) Each has its very specific audience, its unique markets, its industry's dynamics, and even its own tone of voice. At an advertising agency, you can't represent two companies competing in the same industry. So, you have to juggle the logic of multiple industries at the same time. There was always something new to learn and master.

Creatively, you give birth to new artistic babies every day. Ads and commercials are very transient things. They live or die upon presentation. And should they live to be produced, once out in the world, their life on the air or in the newspaper is very short. Today, you're dominating a full page of the newspaper. Tomorrow, that paper is wrapping fish. Advertising is disposable. As soon as one project is done, you're working on another. The wonderful result is that you're never bored.

The third wonderful thing is that advertising opens the door to meeting and working with people you admire. If I wanted to work with a movie star, a rock star, or a political star, I could. If I wanted to work with Joe DiMaggio, I could — and I did. That's the topic of my next story.

To be fair, I didn't decide I was going to work with Joe DiMaggio first and then find a client that he was appropriate for. We were working for Pfizer on a ground-breaking product that cured athlete's foot. (Not very glamorous but quite important if you have itchy feet.)

We wanted a major a star-athlete to represent it. There are a handful of athletes who transcend their sport. Rarely are they elevated to the rank of "American Hero." Joe DiMaggio was one such hero. Paul Simon didn't write, *"Where have you gone,* Yogi Berra? *Our nation turns its lonely eyes to you."* It was Joe. He had the kind of credibility that few athletes had. And somehow, we were able to hire him.

The idea behind the commercial was simple. This wasn't an athlete promoting a watch. This was an athlete discussing an ailment that had been the bane of every athlete's daily existence. Athletes, by the nature of what they do, are using shared locker room showers daily and are constantly exposed to the athlete's foot fungus. It's an issue for us non-athletes, but the condition is not typically chronic.

In the commercial, Joe talks about his lifelong battle with the ailment and introduces the first product to actually cure it. Nothing earth-shaking in its presentation, but he's very believable. For an ailment that had never had a cure, this is big news, and believability is not easily established.

I worked with Joe for a solid week. The one thing I was told before I met Joe was that there was one subject I was forbidden to discuss: Marilyn. And, of course, I didn't. We spent many hours together and talked about everything else; from his life growing up to the evolution of his baseball career.

The thing that surprised me was how completely humble and decent he was. When we were sitting for hours in the mostly empty stadium, sometimes people would stand a section below us and stare at him. When Joe noticed this, he could have simply ignored it or been irritated at being on public display. Instead. he was gracious and inviting.

"I see you have a camera," he would call down. "Come on up. David, would you take his camera and snap a shot for my friend here and me? Tell me your name." If this scene didn't happen 30 times over the five days, it didn't happen once. Joe recognized that he was a seen as a hero. And in his life, he agreed to play the part.

Many, in fact most, celebrities I've worked with are annoyed, sometimes visibly so, when strangers invade their space. It's understandable. This invasion is constant. Strangers will come up when you're eating dinner with slip of paper in hand asking for an autograph or disturb a conversation to say hello and shake your hand. "Oh, I don't mean to interrupt," they say. But that's precisely what they meant to do. If this happened once a day, it might be bearable. For some, this happens once every 10 minutes. Joe took this is stride. That's the price you pay for celebrity.

Instead of spending all day in the stadium seats, Joe showed me about the place between takes. "There is where my locker was, and here's our long-time locker room attendant, Max. Max, say hello to my friend David. Max was always the best." Joe knew everybody and made it his business to remember everybody's name and make them feel important.

One day, he walked me out to home plate. You can't grasp how far away the outfield wall is from the plate until you see it from ground level. After years of thinking I was a pretty good athlete, I realized that on my best day, I couldn't hit it to the deep outfield. A home run? impossible.

"David," Joe points to the roof above the right field stands, "Mickey once hit a ball that bounced off the façade above the third deck." You have no idea how high the top of the third deck is. "He hit it so hard, it caromed to the infield. They say that if it cleared the façade it would have traveled over 700 feet." It's an impressive story. But the most impressive part is DiMaggio didn't regale me about any one of the 148 homers he hit at the stadium—just Mickey's. He was that kind of guy.

The only thing I found that wasn't so heroic about Joe is that he requested a new sport jacket for each day of the shoot. And then, at the end of the shoot he asked to keep them. But Joe is not alone in this. Celebrities are notorious for taking their wardrobe home.

Let me give you another story of even worse celebrity cheapness.

When I lived on 57th Street in Manhattan, my next-door neighbor was Rocky Graziano. Rocky was a Brooklyn kid, and had been the middle-weight boxing champion in 1947. They made a movie about his life, *Somebody Up There Likes Me*. Good film. Rocky was quite a character. We would travel down on the elevator together and over time we became friendly. Not friends, but friendly. This particular night on the elevator, Rocky turned to me and said, "I'm gonna P.J.'s, wanna come?" "Sure," I said. P.J. Clarke's was the legendary bar and restaurant on 55th street and 3rd Avenue and Rocky was a regular. After spending about an hour at the table, several rounds of drinks, and the great burgers they make there, this stranger wanders up.

"Hi Rock, great to meet you. Boy, this is a thrill. I'm one of your biggest fans. Mind if I sit down?"

"No problem," says Rocky.

Now, Rocky doesn't know this guy from a hole in the wall, but he invites him to sit down. Quite gracious, I think. Ten minutes later, before the guy can even order a drink, the check comes and Rocky hands it to him. The guy hasn't had even a drink of water. He pays for all the drinks and food he *didn't* have and leaves. "Great meeting you, Rocky."

I turn to Rocky, "Rocky, how could you give the guy the check?" Rocky replies, "When they sit with the Rock, *they* pay."

One of the sad realities about celebrities is that many have an enormous sense of entitlement. Your hour in the sun with them comes at a price.

The other sad reality is that they rarely live up to who you think — and *hope* — they are. It's easy to confuse the talent and the person. Ironically, some of the saddest people I've ever known are comedians.

Gallo

ONE day at the agency, out of the blue, we received a call from Gallo Brothers—the wine giant from Modesto, California. The call elicited strong emotional reactions from folks at the agency, both positive and negative.

On the positive side, Gallo was a major, big-budget television advertiser. Most recently, their commercials produced by Hal Riney in San Francisco were beautiful, quite poetic, and had won multiple awards for creativity. On the negative side, Gallo had a reputation for being one of the most difficult clients in all of advertising. Other than the Riney work, Gallo had a long history of rather ordinary advertising. So, the question was: Which Gallo was calling?

We'd soon find out.

The caller said that Gallo had been following the work of our agency for some time, and they would like us to come out to Modesto and make a credentials presentation.

What this means, in lay terms, is that they wanted us to show them work we'd created for our other clients which demonstrated our skill at marketing similar kinds of products to theirs and explain the marketing problems these spots solved and their results. This is very standard fare. It is what you put together for any new business presentation.

We asked if they could give us more information about which products in the Gallo stable of wines we were pursuing. "No, we'll tell you about that later—should you pass the credentials presentation. You will then be given a fee for presenting creative executions against the brand you'll learn about. And should the creative work be accepted and produced, you'll be given the account."

This was unusual — the paying for presentation part.

There was a time in the past, when agencies simply made credentials presentations and won an account based upon the impressive work and success they had achieved for other clients. The prospects surmised that what you had done for others, you'd do for them. It's not a wholly far-fetched proposition. But those were the good old days when clients believed in the magic agencies wielded.

Over recent years, more and more clients had said, "Nice work you did for those other guys, but what would you do specifically for me?" At first, agencies charged a large fee for these kinds of presentations and that was appropriate. The presentations contain agency marketing insights on the client's business and, in many cases, creative solutions to the marketing problems discussed. Creating the work demands a lot of time and effort by large numbers of agency personnel. This kind of time and effort is what the agency's ongoing clients pay for. Why should non-clients get it for free?

It didn't take many years for paid, new business presentations to become history. As clients began to ask agencies to compete for their business, in order for one agency to gain an advantage over its competitors, they would offer the work for free. And, of course, the competing agencies would follow suit. "BBDO is a whore, who are you not to be?"

I remember approaching several agencies who were competing with us for a piece of business and said, "What if we all said we would not work for nothing and together we demanded a fee for the pitch." They all thought it was a great idea and agreed. Of the four agencies who agreed, two reneged behind our backs and worked for nothing. Liars? Cheats? I learned over the years that it's par for the course.

Surprisingly, in this everything-for-nothing environment, Gallo was actually offering a fee for our creative presentation and a very sizable fee at that. They were very generous indeed.

As a result, greed got the best of us. We put aside our initial misgivings about Gallo, agreed to go and put together a reel of the high-end and luxury brands that we had had success with.

Then, we headed out to Modesto to meet the Gallos.

When we arrived for the presentation, we were once again surprised. Ernest Gallo himself was in the room along with four of his lieutenants. This was Ernest of Ernest and Julio Gallo. This was not a division president, not a marketing director; this was the man himself. We had never seen the principal of a large company attend a preliminary meeting with an agency. I guess they were serious about this meeting.

The presentation went well. Ernest and his underlings asked intelligent questions about the work we had done for others. They were quite complimentary about it. As the meeting ended, they asked us to take the next step and make a creative presentation, for a huge fee. The fee was larger than the yearly advertising income for several of our smaller accounts.

Was this a different Gallo than the monster we'd always heard about? Had they had a change of heart? Certainly, the Riney work currently running was among the best work in the business. Clearly, they recognized and appreciated good work. With optimism soaring, we went back to New York and set out to create work in the same spirit of excellence as Riney's.

After about eight weeks, we arrived back at Gallo, creative work in hand. We were quite proud of it. It was elegant, emotional, and really fresh. It was work that took the Riney vision a step further — great music, crisp visuals, nice drama. We believe we'd nailed it.

While we waited for the meeting to begin, we chit-chatted for about a half hour with the marketing person who'd been our principal contact up until now. In the middle of our small talk, I asked about the wonderful Riney work that had run earlier in the year. I was wondering why Riney wasn't awarded this new product. Perhaps this was an ill-advised question from an agency that was pursuing the account. I simply wanted to know whether Riney had the inside track on this piece of the business, in which case, all our efforts would be pushed aside. (In the business, this is not unusual.) I was aghast when I learned that Gallo now hated the Riney work and thoroughly disavowed it. Oh, my God. This was the work that had given us incentive to agree to talk to Gallo in the first place.

Had we known the Riney work was in Gallo's opinion a misstep, we never would have come here. It probably meant that they'd hate our work, too.

But we were here, and the work was done. No choice but to move forward.

In a state of bewilderment, we were ushered into a huge conference room. Seated directly across from us were twenty men. *Twenty.* In the center of the group was Ernest, flanked on the left by his head marketing person and long-time consigliere, and on the right by his son, David. To the left and right of them sat eight current and eight former marketing directors.

We'd never seen anything like this before. The eight marketing people on the left had taken the jobs of the eight on the right.

Why were the ex-marketing people there? (Clearly, for a sizable fee.) We imagined the two marketing groups loathed each other and intended to upstage each other. How would they upstage each other? By taking turns eviscerating our work. This was perhaps the most Machiavellian construct I'd ever witnessed.

Can you imagine being one of the current marketing people whose future depended upon besting the former marketing people by trying to be the smartest person at the table? It soon became clear that you got no points for liking something. You went to the head of the class by being the most incisive in your criticism. This was the friendly, supportive group we were to present to.

Ernest announced to us that after we presented each commercial, each person at the table, beginning with the lowest ranking, would comment on the work. Ernest, of course, could interject at any time. We were then told that the agency was forbidden to respond to the multiple comments. We could not explain or defend our work. Clearly, defending or—heaven-forbid disagreeing— was a waste of Gallo's time.

Do you know how hard it is to listen to a stream of demeaning comments and remain quiet? And not leap across the table to strangle someone? This is running the gauntlet without covering your head.

That day, we presented eight commercials. To say each was shredded would be an understatement. The most creativity that day was demonstrated by the Gallo marketing folks who somehow managed to find new faults with each spot without repeating each other's slurs. To be fair, occasionally someone would say something positive about a spot, but such kindnesses were drowned in a sea of sniping. Since I was presenting all this work, I took the full-frontal assault.

To give you a sense of how bad it was, as I was describing the opening scene in one spot with "We open on a table and…" I was six words in and Ernest interrupted me with "We did that three years ago. Next."

"Aren't you interested at what happens at the table next? Is the table in the middle of the Sahara Desert? At the table, are there chimpanzees drinking Gallo out of glass slippers? Is Sophia Loren sitting there naked?" I never got a chance to deliver the second sentence…

"Next."

It was like the joke about sleeping with the 85 year old lifelong prostitute: As you are taking off your pants, she asks, "You got any new ways?" Gallo had seen everything or at least they thought they had.

This was, without question, the most difficult meeting I've ever been in—before or since. And that's saying a lot, because in the advertising business, criticism can be brutal. At the end of our presentation, I looked down to see if I still had my legs.

Finally, Ernest said "Thank you for all the good thinking." Huh?

What a nice thing to say as I was gathering up my body parts. We picked up our storyboards and trudged down the hall toward the car. Before we had a chance to lick our wounds, our friend (who before the meeting had given us the news about the dreadfulness of the Riney work) ran down the hall to stop us. He pulled us into an office and excitedly said, "Wow. This is so exciting. So, when are you guys coming back?"

"Huh", we all said in unison. Didn't he get it? Had he been at a different meeting?

"This was a spectacular first meeting. One of the best we've had in years. There were so many good things," he said. "In the second spot, they liked three lines of copy at the opening. I wrote them down. And what about the music in the fourth spot? And they really liked the sophistication of number eight. There's so much to build on. So, how much time do you need to make the revisions for the next meeting?" This guy actually thought there was something to salvage out of this train wreck.

I didn't know what to say. All I could blurt out was, "Let me get back to you when we get to the office."

We got to the car and drove in stunned silence. I'm thinking to myself, *"Why would I agree to subject the agency to this kind of ugliness?"* Shortly, I asked to stop the car and turned to ask the group:

"So, when are we going back there?"

In unison, we all shouted, "Never!"

And never, it was.

I must say, sitting here recalling this all these years later, I realize I've never fully recovered. That meeting sliced a little chunk of me away. Advertising is not for the thin-skinned.

Boar's Head

I'VE written thus far about some dreadful people and sometimes funny, sometimes frightful events. But every last one wasn't dreadful and every experience wasn't frightful — quite the opposite.

One morning, at the beginning of my agency's life, Alice O'Leary came to my office. Alice was a senior account person at the agency. Alice tells me she has just had a conversation with Marvin Sloves, the founding partner at the agency Scali, McCabe, Sloves. She and Marvin have been close buddies for many years. Marvin tells her that a young fellow by the name of Bob Martin has just left his office. Bob is the son of one of the owners of Boar's Head, the New York-based deli company. Bob was interested in giving Scali, McCabe, Sloves the Boar's Head business, based upon the great work they'd done for Purdue Chicken and Hebrew National hot dogs. Marvin tells Bob he can't take the business because it would be in direct conflict with several of the Purdue products and all of Hebrew National's. While Marvin would love to have Bob's business, he knows his clients would not allow it. Bob asks Marvin whether he has any suggestions for another agency, and he recommends Altschiller Reitzfeld.

The next day, Alice tells us a Bob Martin has called and she has arranged a meeting with the agency. As New Yorkers, we are very familiar with Boar's Head. It is sold mainly in mom-and-pop delicatessens all over New York and has an impeccable reputation for quality, as I would one day write in a headline, "Compromise Elsewhere." But for the life of us, we can't remember ever seeing a commercial or an ad for them. Amazingly, it appears that the Boar's Head brand has been built solely by word of mouth. To attain such a reputation without a penny's worth of advertising is unheard of.

For a young, new agency (we were less than a year old at the time), reputable brand names are what give you credibility and we sure could use some.

When Bob came into the office, we were surprised. He was handsome, about 6 ft., 4 in. tall, but much younger than we had expected, maybe 28 or 30. He was very smart and very passionate about his company.

When he saw our credentials presentation, he was impressed. In fact, he was impressed enough to offer us his account without going back to talk to his team. What we didn't realize was, in the advertising department, there was no "Boar's Head team," just Bob.

Bob laid out a seemingly impossible task.

"You know," he said, "bologna is the by-product of ham." No, we didn't know that.

"The problem is, the more ham we sell, the more trimmings we have to make bologna with. It's a never-ending cycle. What I need you to do is sell tons of Boar's Head bologna without selling tons more ham."

Had I been honest with him, I would have told him, "Bob, that can't be done. As we enhance the reputation of your bologna, we will enhance the reputation of the ham, and the reputation of the brand itself." But we figured if we did a good enough job on the bologna, he'd forgive us if we improved his ham business, too.

Had Bob been completely honest with us, he also would have told us, "No, I'm not giving you this account, I'm hoping you can sell lots of bologna so we can become an account. My father and my uncle don't believe in advertising. They've given me a tiny budget and one opportunity to prove to them that advertising works. You've got one shot. Unless you can prove advertising increases sales in a meaningful way, we're gone from your agency, and we're out of the advertising business."

Frankly, had Bob told us all this, we would not have taken the assignment. At an agency, getting up to speed on an account is a major learning experience. This costs an agency a lot of staff time and therefore, a lot of money. Taking a flyer on a bologna bonanza and hitting a home run on your first time at bat is not a good business bet. But since the agency was treading water, we jumped in with both feet.

We instantly loved Bob's aggressive, positive attitude. Unlike most clients we had met, he was willing to tilt windmills.

Bob gave us all sorts of facts about his bologna and how it was made. He really knew the deli business. Also important, Bob gave us all sorts of information about how poorly other hams and bolognas were made. All the terrible things that Boar's Head left out, the leading brands put in. Ugh.

Over the next several meetings amongst ourselves, as we began to think about the deli business, a light bulb went off—we had a truly interesting insight. Then, based upon that insight, we did a little research. Actually, we went out and talked to a handful of people. Not enough people to call it "research" really. This was done on a shoestring, but if we were right about the insight, we could get someplace.

We had a strong feeling that people didn't trust the quality of deli products, particularly bologna. They thought that it was mystery meat. And the more people we asked, the more they confirmed this.

Up until this point, in the deli business, (in fact, in the food business) brands were not built on quality, but on taste. Why is it delicious? How delicious?

"Forget what's in it—it's delicious."

There was so much emphasis on delicious that the word "delicious" had become almost meaningless. At the time, there were lots of jingles, lots of cute children, lots of smiles and smacking of lips. Remember, "My bologna has a first name, it's O-S-C-A-R"?

We wanted none of that inanity. What we had to say became clear to us: Boar's Head is of impeccable quality. But even more important, it isn't simply that Boar's Head bologna is really good, it's that all the other stuff is really crap. We were to position ourselves as the exception to the quality compromises other deli products made.

We believed that the ugly admission about the overall lack of quality in the category would make our quality claim believable.

The question was, did we have a client with big enough balls to take on the industry?

Would he be willing to expose his competitors for all the awful things they put in their bologna? Was he worried that they'd sue him or come after Boar's Head with budgets 100 times larger than his? He didn't worry for a second or if he did, he never showed it. When Bob heard the idea and saw the advertising that supported it, he leapt at it. This guy feared nothing.

We created a full-page newspaper ad, a radio spot, and a beautiful TV commercial that cost a nickel. (That's all that Boar's Head had.)

How did we get a TV spot produced on a shoestring budget? Well, we didn't try to create the war of the worlds on chump change. We visualized something exceptionally simple: bologna being sliced on a slicer, shot in super slow motion, and falling balletically through the air and eventually landing on a sandwich. Then, we approached one of the great still food photographers to shoot it on film. Because he was a friend, and because he needed film credits, we induced him to do it for practically nothing. Henry Sandbank shot the commercial for $10,000 including editing and music. If it were done today, it would cost half a million.

While the viewer was watching this mesmerizingly beautiful cascading bologna, the announcer told us all the things that this bologna didn't have in it—no strange parts, no fillers, no mysterious chemicals. It ended intoning "Boar's Head. Pure bologna. Not phony baloney."

When it went on the air, the result was instantaneous. Sales of the bologna soared the day it ran, and sales rose week after week. It took little time for there to be no question to Bob's father and uncle that advertising worked. And there was also no question that the story of uncompromising quality worked.

Boar's Head began to advertise its bologna in other cities. Following the success of bologna, over the next few years we created advertising for ham, then roast beef, then turkey, then chicken, then an endless variety of cheeses. In market after market, Boar's Head proved that a conscientious adherence to quality worked. The pronouncement that the competition was crappy, was profoundly potent.

End of story: It's been 40 years since Bob Martin walked into our fledgling agency's doors. In that time, Boar's Head has become the most highly regarded deli company in America. The brand is more well-known, and more prestigious than deli companies many times its size. Over the years, scores of agencies came knocking on Boar's Head's door to pitch what was now a very large account. Bob turned down every single one. When I decided to sell my agency and retire, Bob opted out of the sale, so I could start a new agency with Boar's Head as its star client. How do you retire with a client like that?

This is my second retirement.

Advertising is an ugly, fickle business. Loyalty is never a consideration. Clients stay at an agency an average of less than three years. I've been creating the advertising for Boar's Head for more than ten times that. We've been together longer, in fact, than just about any client and agency in the history of the business. Who knows, we may hold the Guinness World Record. Today, having finally retired, I'm on their board.

The work we produced was made possible because Bob Martin was courageous enough to allow it to live and pushed us to question limits at every turn. He was the first to say that he owed much of his company's monumental success to the advertising we had created. Not too many clients like that. He's one of a kind.

Epilogue

MY career and the stories in this book took place in what advertising historians call "The Golden Age of Advertising."

The first questions to ask, I guess, are why and when did this Golden Age begin and when and why did it end? And what the hell is a "Golden Age" anyway?

This will hopefully explain where the advertising business is now compared to what it was then — at least in my estimation.

So, let's talk about when the Golden Age began.

I guess if you had to put a date on it, it would be during the tail end of 1950s or the early 1960s — just before I entered the business.

It began, in part, because of the birth of the modern TV commercial. In the fifties, commercials were mainly "standups." A spokesperson in a TV studio stood in front of the camera, yapping about a box of cereal or a can of soup, or in the case of Betty Furness and Ronald Reagan, hawking a refrigerator. The reason that people were standing like cardboard cutouts is that TV cameras were huge and relatively immobile. The quality of the commercial was poor because it was a recording of a TV monitor onto motion picture film. Something they called a kinescope — essentially a video of a video. As technology advanced and allowed film to replace kinescope, cameras became portable, commercials could be shot outside the TV studio, and they finally began to look like movies.

More important than the technological advances in TV and still photography, there was a dramatic change in the tone of voice of ads and commercials.

As we discussed earlier in this book, in the late `50s an advertising agency emerged that would dramatically change the industry. The agency was called Doyle Dane Bernbach. Bill Bernbach, its creative director, opened a door to humor, wit, and humanity that simply hadn't existed in ads or commercials before. I won't wax poetic about him again here, but the debt we owe to him is immeasurable.

Within a few years, DDB gave birth to a host of advertising agency acolytes. The proliferation of these agencies, and the emergence of agencies that were the children of these, gave birth to the advertising renaissance they call the "Golden Age."

Mind you, this new voice never took over the industry entirely. For the most part, the packaged goods businesses stayed tied to the old vision. So, commercials became a mixed bag. Some were brilliant and some were dated and mediocre. But the new genre of ads and commercials so overshadowed the old, it was as if a creative window had opened. The Golden Age had begun.

How then did this Golden Age turn to brass? How did we go from the advertising renaissance to where we are today? There are many reasons, but two stand out to me.

In the '60s, the client was often the founder of a company. He was not a marketing MBA; he was an entrepreneur and often, a visionary. Think Steve Jobs. He was willing to take risks and since he had not grown up in advertising, he was willing to entrust commercial messaging to the agency. I remember Carl Ally telling these prospective clients, "We are the doctor. You need to put yourself in our hands," and they actually believed it.

But by the 1990s, the client/CEO had kicked himself upstairs and relegated marketing to the "marketing experts." Often, they were ex-agency marketing people. Power had moved from the agency side to the client side. Decision-making was now in the hands of marketing pseudo-scientists and out of the hands of agency creatives. Insight (and humor) gave way to pragmatic judgment.

At this same time, small agencies began to sell themselves to larger agencies. It began with English conglomerates gobbling up U.S. entities. Then, American agencies began to devour each other. The motivation for all this buying and selling was that owners of the agencies could cash out and become wealthy, and buyers could dramatically increase their bottom line in the public stock exchanges. (Today three advertising conglomerates control the industry.)

Now, here's the important fact about the end of the Golden Age: In order for the big agencies to pay for gobbling up the small agencies, their business model demanded that the agency that was purchased had to pay for itself over a short period of years out of its profits. The hope and expectation here was that the small agency would grow fast enough to have enough profit to pay the debt. But often, that simply didn't happen; either the buyer had overpaid, or the agency underperformed.

So how did the investor get his money out of the agency he'd purchased? The solution was inevitable—cut staff. Because creative people were generally the highest paid group, you'd cut the creative people. Or, replace high-priced, more experienced writers and art directors with juniors, even beginners. You could have a cheap boatload of them working under a few high-paid supervisors. Then, give the seniors little time to supervise. Or put fewer creative people on a project and ask them to come up with creative solutions in a fraction of the time they previously had. Or fire full-time creatives and replace them with freelancers who could be fired without notice. "Here, work a week on this problem. I'll give you a half hour of background. Then, give me a handful of ads or commercials and bye-bye." (You should note that advertising agencies led the way in the gig economy.)

With less time to create and fewer experienced creators, the accomplishment was simply getting the work—any work—out on time for a meeting. Without sufficient motivation to relentlessly strive for great work, mediocrity was inevitable.

So here we are, twenty years later. Have you seen many truly exciting commercials on TV lately? The Super Bowl used to be a place you could count on. Can you think of a single Super Bowl commercial that has come up in conversation lately?

How about ads? When you open a magazine—if you still open a magazine—is there a campaign that pops out? Think hard.

The business simply ain't what it used to be. This is not sour grapes from some geezer. Track down anyone you know who is in business today and ask:

"Are you excited by what you see in advertising these days?"

Not a chance.

As I reflect back, I must admit that I was really, really lucky.

I was in the right place at the right time; working in a short-lived, but an extraordinarily creative era in the history of advertising. I was writing ads and commercials at one of the greatest agencies of that era. The work I was able to produce there allowed me to open my own agency and continue to do the work that I love for 40 years.

I remember my good friend, a brilliant art director, saying, "I can't believe it. They actually pay me for what I'd do for free."

Can't ask for more than that.

CPSIA information can be obtained
at www.ICGtesting.com
Printed in the USA
BVHW072200021121
620543BV00003B/188